SHOULD TEXTBOOKS CHALLENGE STUDENTS?

The Case for Easier or Harder Textbooks

SHOULD TEXTBOOKS CHALLENGE STUDENTS?

The Case for Easier or Harder Textbooks

Jeanne S. Chall
and
Sue S. Conard

with Susan Harris-Sharples

Teachers College, Columbia University
New York and London

Published by Teachers College Press, 1234 Amsterdam Avenue New York, NY 10027

Library of Congress Cataloging-in-Publication Data
Chall, Jeanne Sternlicht, 1921–
  Should textbooks challenge students? : the case for easier or
harder textbooks / Jeanne S. Chall and Sue S. Conard with Susan
Harris-Sharples.
     p.   cm.
  Includes bibliographical references (p.   ) and index.
  ISBN 0-8077-3065-3 (cloth : alk. paper). — ISBN 0-8077-3064-5
(alk. paper : pbk.)
  1. Textbooks — United States — Readability.   2. Textbooks — United
States — Evaluation.   I. Conard, Sue S.   II. Harris-Sharples, Susan.   III. Title.
LB3045.8.C47   1991
371.3′2 — dc20   91-11359

Printed on acid-free paper

Manufactured in the United States of America

98   97   96   95   94   93   92   91   8   7   6   5   4   3   2   1

Contents

v

Preface

This book is based on a study of textbooks begun early in the 1980s and updated through 1989. It is concerned with the influence of textbooks on students' learning of content and their reading development over time. Specifically, we have been interested in aspects of text that contribute to the ease or difficulty of understanding what is read.

When we began the study, we found relatively little general attention paid to the topic among educational researchers and practitioners, although it has been an area of concern for some researchers and cognitive and developmental psychologists for at least 50 years. By the middle 1980s, however, many researchers as well as educational planners, publishers, and curriculum developers became engaged in a widespread and often heated debate about the level of difficulty that constitutes an optimal match between texts and readers. The almost universal consensus maintained from the 1920s through the 1970s that textbooks were too difficult changed dramatically to a growing uneasiness that textbooks might not be challenging enough.

It is during such a time of change and uncertainty that our study may be of particular value. It can help explain why textbooks have become easier over the last half-century, what the evidence was for making the books easier, and what new evidence exists for making them more difficult.

In essence, this book presents both our research findings and our findings on the practices and preferences of teachers, students, and educational publishers on factors relating to difficulty. Our hope is that these findings may make possible more rational decisions on textbook development, selection, and use. The book is addressed to editors and publishers, to textbook-adoption committees, to curriculum developers, to teachers at the elementary and high school levels, and to parents and others who are concerned with the role of textbooks in the education of young people.

Various methods were used to answer the relevant questions, including a review of the published literature, a sampling survey of the opinions of publishers and teachers, and analyses of textbooks and teacher's manuals and methods books for the teaching of reading and content subjects. We observed how textbooks were used in classrooms and asked teachers their opinions about textbooks. We tested students' comprehension of textbook passages and interviewed them concerning their preferences.

Many people made our study possible. We wish to thank the Spencer Foundation, and especially H. Thomas James, President, and Marion Faldet, Vice President, for their sustained interest and generous support. A special thanks is due to Ralph W. Tyler for reading the early draft of our research plan and for his helpful suggestions.

James R. Squire of Silver Burdett & Ginn was a great source of help throughout our work, especially in the selection of representative textbooks to be analyzed.

Our colleague, Helen Popp, was particularly helpful in the development of the research design for classroom observations and student testing. We are also grateful to Marcus Lieberman for the statistical analyses and to Carol Weiss and Julie Wilson, who assisted us in the construction of questionnaires.

Many of our graduate students assisted in the collection and analysis of data: Peter Thacker was especially helpful in observing in the high school classrooms; Barbara Eckhoff, in the analysis of elementary and high school textbooks; Dorothy Henry, in the recording and preparing of data for analysis; Loriana Novoa, in the analysis of teacher education methods textbooks; Ann Rosebery, in the analysis of teacher's manuals for social studies and science; and Beth Warren, in the analysis of responses from textbook-adoption committees. Updates of analyses and literature reviews were conducted by Barbara Kraemer, Mary Lou Adams, Elizabeth Nolan, and Mary Lawlor, who also assisted with the bibliography and editing the appendixes.

This study would not have been possible without the full cooperation of the educational publishers and teachers who responded to our questionnaires and of the school personnel who welcomed us into their classrooms and talked with us about their experiences and preferences. We are also grateful to the students who participated in the testing and shared with us their comments and preferences. We extend special thanks to Bernard Schulman, Superintendent of Schools, and Fred Burnaby and Dorothy Lally, Directors of Reading, who made our school-based research fruitful and extremely pleasant.

Our warmest thanks are also extended to David Weaver, formerly of the Association of American Publishers, and to the late Mary McNulty, who assisted us in those aspects of the study that required the involvement of educational publishers.

Our warm appreciation is extended, also, to Ann Cura, who, with her characteristic care and efficiency, oversaw the research project from beginning to end; and to Faith Harvey and Andrea Nuttila, who typed the final manuscript.

While we are mindful of the assistance from many, we are equally mindful that the responsibility for the book is our own.

SHOULD TEXTBOOKS CHALLENGE STUDENTS?

The Case for Easier or Harder Textbooks

CHAPTER 1

Introduction: Growing Concerns About Textbooks

In the United States, the publishing of textbooks is a billion-dollar enterprise. Textbooks are sold to tens of thousands of schools and used in classrooms by millions of teachers and tens of millions of students. By the time most students complete high school, they will have been exposed to over 32,000 pages in textbooks. Almost all of their time in reading instruction and at least three-fourths of their time in content classes will be spent with a textbook (Black, 1967; Chall & Squire, 1991; EPIE Institute, 1976; Hoffman & Roser, 1987; Komoski, 1978; Squire, 1988).

Textbooks have been and continue to be pervasive in U.S. schools. Yet, until the early 1980s, public concern with textbooks was fairly limited. Even in the schools, they were so much an accepted part of classroom life that they went almost unnoticed. Until quite recently, most school improvement efforts virtually ignored them or simply took them for granted (Woodward, 1986).

Although educational researchers have long been interested in textbooks, Squire (1988) notes that only a few have carried this interest beyond single, isolated studies. In fact, the number of published works on textbooks is relatively limited.

In 1918, A. L. Hall-Quest described in his preface to *The Textbook: How to Use and Judge It* how the writing of the book had been the effort of a "pioneer in a dark and unknown wilderness" (p. vii). Even after an exhaustive search, he could find no other books about textbooks. His call for the scholarly consideration of textbooks seemed to go unheeded, since many decades later, at a 1975 conference on the status of textbooks sponsored by the Library of Congress and the National Institute of Education, D. F. Walker echoed this concern and expressed amazement that there were still so few serious works on the subject (see Walker, 1981, for a published account of his views of the conference).

Shortly after this conference was convened, however, two studies about textbooks were published that seemed to catch the attention of the nation and to arouse the kind of sustained interest both Hall-Quest and Walker had urged. The first, an analysis of American history books by historian Frances FitzGerald, was serialized in the *New Yorker* magazine and later published in book form (1979). It called into question the content of these books and documented their growing tendency toward vacuousness and blandness, as well as the lack of a sustained, single voice. The second study, by Chall, Conard, and Harris (1977), was prepared for the Advisory Panel on the Scholastic Aptitude Test Score Decline and commissioned by the College Board and Educational Testing Service. It provided the impetus for the work we report here. The study was one of more than twenty undertaken to explain the precipitous decline of SAT scores since 1963, especially verbal scores.

The approach we took in our study (Chall et al., 1977) was to compare the difficulty of textbooks (using quantitative and qualitative measures) with changes in the scores. We hypothesized that students' verbal SAT scores would be positively related to variations in the difficulty of the textbooks used in reading, composition, social studies, and literature at specific points (cohorts) in their 11 years of schooling.

Indeed, we found compelling evidence of an association between the lowering of students' SAT scores and the declining difficulty of their books (Chall et al., 1977). Essentially, students who were enrolled in elementary and secondary schools when more difficult textbooks were used had higher verbal SAT scores; when easier textbooks were used, students had lower scores.

We also found a trend of decreasing difficulty in the most widely used textbooks over the 30-year period from 1945 to 1975 (Chall et al., 1977). On the whole, the later the copyright dates of textbooks for the same grade, the easier they were, as measured by indices of readability level, maturity level, difficulty of questions, and extent of illustration. In the reading textbooks in particular, another indicator was whether the selection was written expressly for the book. By the eleventh grade, most of the textbooks used during the years of the SAT decline — 1963 to 1975 — were about 1 to 2 years below the average reading abilities of the students and about 2 or more years below the readability levels of the SAT test passages. This evidence suggested that probably more than half of the students who took the test during the 1960s and 1970s were using textbooks below their reading levels and may not have been sufficiently challenged (Chall et al., 1977). We hypothesized, further, that the decreasing challenge of the textbooks would likely have a stronger negative influence on the progress of students who came from lower socioeconomic backgrounds since additional reading materials of advanced difficulty would probably be found less frequently in their homes than in the homes of more affluent students.

Our findings (Chall et al., 1977) also tended to confirm those from earlier research on the effects of textbook difficulty, namely, that difficulty of textbooks and other instructional materials influences how much students learn from texts (Chall, 1958; Klare, 1963, 1974–1975). (See Chapter 2 for a review of the literature on this topic.) What seemed to be a relatively new finding, however, was the cumulative effect of text difficulty on reading development from the first grade through high school. An optimal level of reading difficulty of texts used throughout students' schooling was found to contribute positively to the development of their reading ability as well as to the learning of the subject matter of the various texts.

The advisory panel included these findings in its comprehensive report (College Entrance Examination Board, 1977) and cited them as "clearly discernable evidence" of the "lowering of the demand level of textbooks" and of the declining rigor of the "mastery of skills and knowledge" (p. 47).

Reviews of our study appeared in the *New York Times*, the *Los Angeles Times*, and other newspapers and national magazines. We were invited to present the findings to the annual meetings of the Association of American Publishers and of psychological and educational research associations, and to meetings on textbooks at the Library of Congress and others at the Office of Education. It appeared as if the educational community, educational publishers, and the public were coming to realize, as we had at the conclusion of the study, that textbooks "should be considered as possible direct means of educational innovation and improvement" (Chall et al., 1977, p. 65).

In 1980, the Spencer Foundation provided a grant for us to continue our study into the issue of text difficulty, exploring ways of improving what is learned from texts and improving the effects of textbooks on the development of students' reading. This book reports the findings of our 3-year undertaking, together with additional research that brings the original findings up to date.

Our study was begun at a time when long-standing ideas about textbooks were beginning to be reexamined and reevaluated. On the issue of suitable difficulty, it seemed as if the consensus of the previous 50 years that "the easier the textbook, the better" was changing (at least in the recommendations of educational reform groups) to "the harder, the better." Thus we sought to synthesize the existing research evidence on suitable difficulty and also to find out why it had been possible to draw such strikingly different conclusions from it at different times. We tried, therefore, to understand the many forces that influenced the research on textbooks, as well as those related to their development, selection, and use.

We used many different kinds of research methods: analyses and syntheses of the relevant literature; surveys of the opinions of publishers, teachers, and curriculum specialists; and analyses of widely used textbooks for reading, social studies, and science for the elementary and high school grades. We tested students' reading and understanding of selections from their textbooks and requested their views and preferences. We analyzed textbooks written for prospective teachers on methods of teaching reading and other subjects, and the teacher's manuals accompanying textbooks, and we surveyed textbook-adoption committees. These procedures were all related to the broader purpose of learning more about textbook difficulty and the level of challenge that is most effective for the learning of content and for students' reading development during the elementary and high school years.

DEFINITION OF TERMS

What is meant by *suitable difficulty*, or *optimal challenge*? The difficulty of written materials can best be viewed as occurring on a continuum ranging from very easy to very hard for the population of readers as a whole, both children and adults. Simply put, comic books are usually easier in this sense than most news magazines and newspapers, because more people can read the former. A local newspaper is generally easier than a professional periodical such as the *New England Journal of Medicine*, also by virtue of the fact that more people can read the newspaper.

Similarly, textbooks can be placed on a continuum of difficulty ranging from primers to advanced college texts, using the same criterion. The difficulty of textbooks can also be viewed in relation to the reading abilities of those who are expected to read them. A third-grade book is difficult for most second graders but easy for most fourth graders, and it is an easy book for most people in the general population. Thus the easiest or hardest books in a general sense may be easy or hard in terms of reader ability. *Suitable difficulty* thus refers to an optimal match between text and reader.

When difficulty is viewed in relation to student ability, we can also speak of challenge. Thus a challenging textbook is one that is somewhat beyond the reading ability of the reader. It requires some effort and usually some instruction or aid from a teacher or a more able peer. *Appropriate* or *optimal challenge* refers to a best possible fit between the level of the text, the ability of the student, and the instruction available.

One can estimate text difficulty from its internal features, such as frequency of unfamiliar vocabulary, difficulty of content or concepts, complexity of syntax, organization, and cohesiveness. (See Chapter 2.) Indeed, it has been possible for nearly 70 years to use text features to predict the reading comprehension difficulty of texts in terms of the reading abilities needed to read and understand them.

THE PUBLIC DEBATE ON TEXTBOOKS

Shortly after the publication of the College Entrance Examination Board (CEEB) report (1977), other educational researchers and policy makers began to consider the possibility that the challenge level of textbooks could have considerable influence on the improvement of educational achievement at the elementary and high school levels.

In 1983, the National Commission on Excellence in Education (NCEE) concluded that textbooks had been "written down" and recommended in its widely disseminated report, *A Nation at Risk*, that "[these] and other tools of learning and teaching be upgraded to assure more rigorous content" and that "states and school districts should evaluate texts and other materials on their ability to present rigorous and challenging material clearly" (p. 28).

In a relatively short period of time, the idea that the "declining difficulty" of textbooks may have had negative effects on students' learning became widespread. Journalists as well as educators described textbooks as being "dumbed down," a slogan that caught the public's imagination and united various textbook critics (Cody, 1986). Publishers were accused of lowering academic requirements by "oversimplifying," "blanding down," and "watering down" their textbooks, in addition to "writing down" and "dumbing down" (Fiske, 1987).

It should be noted that most critics of textbook difficulty did not seem to rely on relevant research evidence as support for their views. Although our initial study (Chall et al., 1977) had been available for some time, it was seldom mentioned; rather, the various critics seemed to take the position that the decline in rigor of texts was a foregone conclusion and that restoring texts to an earlier level of difficulty would automatically improve achievement. Also missing from these criticisms was any mention of the earlier consensus that had existed for more than 50 years among textbook publishers, teachers, and many educational researchers, that the easier the textbook, the better.

Difficulty and challenge have not been the only aspects of textbooks to be caught up in the growing controversy. From the late 1970s through the mid-1980s, almost all attributes of textbooks have come under attack.

Their perceived shortcomings have been chronicled increasingly in special television features and lead articles in highly regarded periodicals such as *The Christian Science Monitor* and *The New York Times*.

Some of the questions raised have centered around social content. Organizations representing minorities and women demanded more realistic ethnic and gender balance, and other special-interest organizations called for fair representation of the aging and handicapped. Religious fundamentalists lobbied for history books that emphasized traditional values such as patriotism and morality and for biology books that devoted more space to creationism and less to evolution. The most recent of these charges have concerned issues just beginning to awaken in the nation's consciousness, such as the treatment of the environment and the ecological system and the state of the public's health and fitness.

Curricular content has been another target for attack. What should be taught in textbooks? To what extent should each topic be taught? California, one of the largest textbook-adoption states, has led the drive to replace stories written explicitly for reading textbooks with unabridged literary classics. The content of history books has been challenged by the contention that a corpus of historical events that should be known by every "culturally literate" citizen has not always been fully covered in American history textbooks (Hirsch, 1987). Others have argued that textbooks attempt to cover too many topics, berating them for the practice that has come to be called "mentioning" (Tyson-Bernstein & Woodward, 1989).

Another critical thrust has concerned the "tone" of textbooks, judged in terms of their literary style. Many were seen as "unemotional" or "lacking spirit." FitzGerald's *America Revised* (1979) paved the way for attacks on the dullness and homogeneity of "managed" textbooks written by committees rather than by individuals with a strong, singular voice. Complaints of a similar nature about elementary and junior high school history and social studies books were registered in the subsequent studies of Sewall (1987), for the Educational Excellence Network, and Gagnon (1987), for the American Federation of Teachers. These have led to the formation of the American Textbook Council, a national consortium to advance the quality of social studies textbooks and all instructional materials.

In this debate, the tendency has been to cite one or more issues as evidence of a decline in textbook quality. In such an atmosphere of discontent, most critics have found it relatively easy to convince the public that textbooks leave much to be desired.

As the decade of the 1980s drew to a close, it seemed as though the public media had put aside their concern for textbook quality. The issue was then claimed by educational professionals — researchers, scholars, and education writers — who began reporting their findings in books and educational journals. Thus, in 1987, a full issue of the *Elementary School Journal* was devoted to reading textbooks, and lead articles on textbooks appeared in *Phi Delta Kappan* and *Educational Leadership*. In fact, there has been a veritable renaissance during the past few years, in scholarly and professional publications on textbooks. Two National Society for the Study of Education yearbooks on textbooks have been published: *From Socrates to Software: The Teacher As Text and the Text As Teacher* (Jackson & Haroutunian-Gordon, 1989) and *Textbooks and Schooling in the United States* (Elliot & Woodward, 1990). Also published within the last few years were *American History Textbooks* (Sewall, 1987), the *Report Card on Basal Readers* (Goodman, Shannon, Freeman, & Murphy, 1988), and *A Conspiracy of Good Intentions: America's Textbook Fiasco* (Tyson-Bernstein, 1988c).

A review of the most recent books and articles on textbooks — those published during the years 1985 to 1989 — reveals an elevated concern with text difficulty, compared to the past, as well as concern with issues studied earlier, such as content, minority representation, the skills taught, literary style, and the textbook-adoption process (see Appendix B–3). The issue of suitable difficulty has a new focus, however. Its proponents do not seem primarily concerned with improving student achievement and reading development. Instead, suitable difficulty seems to have turned into a concern for "literary quality," which, it is claimed, publishers have sacrificed in their quest for easy books. Thus the call is for literary quality, as if that in itself were an essential factor in a textbook's effectiveness as an instrument of learning and literacy development. There is greater concern, overall, for appropriate text content, organization, and cohesion, as well as for physical features — again, with little evidence given that these factors are related to learning. On the whole, the content criticisms are similar to those made a decade earlier by FitzGerald (1979), that the textbooks are too bland, do not take strong positions, and reveal the lack of passion associated with books written by committees. Some "new" observations are that content-area textbooks treat too many topics with insufficient depth, that they are too profusely illustrated, and are too long.

The "new" criticism compared to the "old" of a few years past attests to the continuing contentiousness of issues surrounding textbooks. The interest in the improvement of textbooks continues to be strong, but what seems to be missing is a concern for a greater knowledge base. Unfortunately, the current debate overlooks the accumulated educational research on the issues and tends as well to overlook the need for relevant, updated research.

In the face of so much information and misinformation, this book is intended to contribute both to a synthesis of the past research and to an update from our current findings. We trust that it will also contribute a more accurate awareness of what we already know on the topic and of what needs to be researched further.

The following chapters present a variety of perspectives on textbooks and difficulty. In Chapter 2 we offer an overview of the past research. Chapters 3 and 4 present evidence from a survey of publishers and teachers on the importance of suitable difficulty in developing and selecting suitable textbooks. In Chapter 5 we describe the results of our comparative analysis of content textbooks published during the years 1974 to 1982 and 1986 to 1989, in terms of difficulty, maturity, and the like. Chapter 6 describes how teachers are informed about text difficulty in the manuals that accompany students' textbooks and by methods textbooks for various subjects. Chapter 7 provides an account of the way textbooks are used in classrooms, from our observations of elementary and secondary classrooms. Insights into how well students can read and understand the textbooks they are using and their preferences with regard to optimal difficulty are included in Chapter 8. Chapter 9 focuses on the textbook-adoption process, and Chapter 10 presents our major conclusions and recommendations.

CHAPTER 2

Research on Text Difficulty: A Historical Review

The events of the past 70 years concerning text difficulty have about them a sense of drama and irony, the stuff of fables and cautionary tales. The early research, begun in the 1920s by some of the most distinguished psychologists and educators, was welcomed with great promise as a means for improving education. Indeed, the constructive outcomes were many. Yet, within a single decade and continuing well into the 1970s, we find evidence that this research was often misunderstood and frequently misused.

This chapter presents a historical review of the research and theory on text difficulty. It considers the instruments that were developed to measure difficulty, how they have been used, and how they have influenced practice. It further considers how practice has influenced the research that was undertaken.

Empirical studies are presented first, followed by relevant theory. Since the research on text difficulty is voluminous, we include here only the most significant studies and trends.

EMPIRICAL RESEARCH

Empirical studies of text difficulty began with two parallel approaches: the study of vocabulary difficulty and the study of comprehension difficulty, or readability.

Vocabulary studies came first, in the early 1920s at the beginning of the scientific movement in education, an era characterized by the search for objective means of answering theretofore elusive questions. Researchers whose particular interest lay in predicting the difficulty of textbooks found a solution in Thorndike's frequency word counts of the English language, published in 1921 and 1931. In addition to ranking words according to

9

their frequency in print, these lists estimated the school grade at which the words should be taught. Along with others modeled after them, Thorndike's lists soon became the primary criterion for grading textbooks. There were other measures of vocabulary as well, for example, the number of "new" or difficult words introduced and the number of times they were repeated. Findings from these word-count studies provided the basis for conclusions about the vocabulary "load" or "burden" of textbooks, particularly textbooks for reading instruction in the primary grades.

The study of readability also began with a concern for textbook difficulty, but its primary interest was in content textbooks and other materials written for older students and adults. In a broad sense, "readability" came to stand for the characteristics of texts that made them more or less "readable" for given groups of readers. These qualities have included interest, legibility, and ease of comprehension (Chall, 1958). With time, readability researchers tended to focus primarily on comprehension difficulty, for which vocabulary measures adopted from the vocabulary studies proved to be strong and consistent predictors. The more difficult the vocabulary, the more difficult the text. Beyond vocabulary, most studies found syntactic features such as sentence length, sentence complexity, and the use of prepositional phrases or clauses to be predictive of readability. The frequency of use of personal pronouns was also a strong predictor, but was used less often. The largest number of factors — 82 — was studied by Gray and Leary in 1935, from their interviews with readers and experts, but they later reduced this number to only four categories: those related to properties of words, sentences, paragraphs, and entire sections.

From the factors identified, readability researchers soon developed mathematical formulas that measured text factors reliably and predicted with considerable validity the difficulty of written materials in relation to the reading ability of intended readers. These instruments came to be known as "readability formulas." By the early 1960s at least 50 readability formulas had been developed (Klare, 1963), and more recent accounts put that number closer to 100 (Klare, 1979). Thus, although the emphases of vocabulary and readability studies differed, both research traditions shared a single concern and purpose: to estimate the difficulty of text objectively in order to effect a better match with prospective readers' abilities.

Through the years, readability formulas and word lists have been widely used by educational publishers and teachers to estimate the difficulty of textbooks, tests, and other educational materials and to match textbooks and students. Perhaps it is this wide use that has led to their overapplication and misuse and, particularly in the case of readability formulas, to criticisms and questions of their effectiveness.

GOALS AND FINDINGS OF TWO EARLY STUDIES

Since its beginning over half a century ago, the research on the vocabulary difficulty of textbooks and on readability has grown steadily. Chall (1958), Klare (1963), and Clifford (1978) give comprehensive accounts of the wealth of the research. More recent updates can be found in Chall (1984, 1988). Brief descriptions of two very early seminal studies will serve here as examples of the common purpose of vocabulary and readability research and generally of their similar results.

An early study of vocabulary difficulty conducted in 1928 by Edward Dolch was concerned with the vocabulary demands of elementary-level reading textbooks. Dolch analyzed a sample of reading textbooks used in the first through fourth grades. Using several vocabulary measures, including range of vocabulary, rate of introducing new words, repetitions of these new words, and the difficulty of the words based on a word list, he found great variation in the vocabulary load of the books for each grade, with as few as 20% and as many as 40% of the words included in the books for each grade unknown to students.

Since elementary teachers found most reading textbooks too hard for their students, and since no research evidence was available on an optimal vocabulary load, Dolch recommended the use of the average of the percentages he had found as a standard both for selecting and for writing new books.

Vocabulary difficulty was also a factor studied in the earliest of readability studies. In 1923, Bertha Lively and S. W. Pressey were approached by junior high school science teachers who were troubled by the difficulty of textbooks, particularly with regard to the number of technical terms they presented. The teachers felt that the study of science was becoming primarily a matter of mastering vocabulary rather than of learning scientific facts and generalizations. They needed an objective way to measure the difficulty of their books in order to select those most appropriate for their students. The researchers studied the problem by arranging 11 books and one local newspaper in what they judged to be an order of increasing difficulty and then measuring various vocabulary characteristics, including the number of different words per thousand, an index based on Thorndike's (1921, 1931) word lists, and the number of highly technical words. The aspects of vocabulary difficulty were compared with the difficulty of the texts, and the first readability formula—essentially an index that predicted a book's difficulty on a scale from easier to harder—was developed.

Common to the vocabulary and readability studies conducted during these early years was the finding that textbooks in most subjects and for most grades were too difficult for the majority of students using them.

WHY THE GREAT CONCERN FOR TEXTBOOK DIFFICULTY?

The concern for appropriate text difficulty that was found in these vocabulary and readability studies was, in many respects, prompted by changing social conditions in schools and in society. Beginning in the 1920s, more students than ever before were attending secondary schools, and these "new" students were often the first in their families to do so. At the same time, the textbooks being used had been written for an earlier generation, a more select population of young people who had stronger academic backgrounds and who were expected to continue their education through college. Thus, a mismatch existed between the students and their texts.

The characteristics of younger students were more stable during these years, since compulsory schooling for elementary-age children had been in effect for some time. However, concern for difficulty at this level may also have been associated with a "new" school population: the children of immigrant families whose proficiency with the English language was relatively limited. We know that many more of these children were entering school during the 1920s, although they are not mentioned in the early research studies on textbooks.

Another possible reason for increased attention to text difficulty in the elementary grades was the shift from an approach emphasizing phonics or decoding to one emphasizing sight words or meaning. The vocabulary in books used in meaning-based beginning reading instruction was restricted so that students had adequate time and exposure to learn a basic core of words. This hypothesis is supported by historical perspectives of vocabulary changes in reading textbooks. The number of different words in primary reading textbooks, for example, decreased substantially from the 1920s through the early 1960s, a time when sight-word or meaning-based methods were prevalent. In contrast, from the late 1960s to the early 1980s, a time when decoding-based methods were more popular, the number of different words in primary reading books increased (see Chall, 1967, 1983a, 1989).

Changing priorities in the larger society may also have encouraged concerns for suitable difficulty. Chief among these was the growing consensus that education should be provided for all children—those of low-income and low-education background, as well as those from more privileged social strata. The idea of universal education was widely embraced by both schools and educational researchers, but accomplishing it proved problematic. Many students could not keep up with the assignments in their textbooks because they were too difficult. The obvious solution was to develop or select easier textbooks so that they could be read by all students within each grade, or at least by as many as could be reasonably expected. Thus, the mission to make instruction meaningful for all students may also have contributed to the lessening of difficulty of the curricula and of textbooks.

THE INFLUENCE OF RESEARCH ON TEXT DIFFICULTY

The influence that this early research had on educational practice was almost immediate. Although the evidence came mainly from comparing texts to each other and from estimating difficulty from various measures of vocabulary, the new books, grade for grade, were easier than the older ones. A rare attempt to correlate reading difficulty with educational outcome was the series of experiments by A. I. Gates (1930) on the effects of different vocabulary loads on students of different abilities. From these experiments he estimated the number of word repetitions needed by first-grade students to achieve mastery of first-grade reading: 30 to 35 for average students, 20 for above-average students, and at least 40 repetitions for students with below-average IQs (see Chall, 1958). In other words, students with IQ scores from 60 to 69 needed three times as many repetitions of words in their textbooks as those with IQ scores from 120 to 129.

Following the Gates (1930) study, first-grade reading textbooks became increasingly easier, using more word repetitions and fewer new words. Although most reading textbooks met Gates's specifications by the late 1930s, later editions of primary reading texts continued to have fewer and fewer new words until the 1960s (Chall, 1988). This trend was generally regarded as positive, although there were a few strong words of warning. These came from renowned professors and researchers such as Gerald Yoakam from the University of Pittsburgh. In 1945, Yoakam wrote, "There is danger that in following the popular appeal of books that are easily readable by children, we shall swing to the other extreme and make books so easy that children will not make desirable progress in the development of vocabulary and in the improvement of their reading power" (p. 307). Later, upon discovering that third-grade students knew most of the words in fourth-grade reading textbooks before they even used them, A. I. Gates (1961) admonished, "Vocabulary controls may have been carried so far as to be useless, if not disadvantageous" (p. 81).

In spite of these cautions and others (see Chall, 1958, 1967; Hockett, 1938; Hockett & Neely, 1937), the vocabularies of reading textbooks continued to decline through the mid-1960s. With each copyright date, most reading textbooks for each elementary grade became easier as publishers competed with one another and with their own earlier editions for books with ever more limited vocabularies.

The reading difficulty of content textbooks was also influenced by research findings. Early studies concluded that content textbooks were also too hard, and recommendations for easier books followed. Accordingly, changes in the difficulty of these books paralleled those of the reading textbooks, but the move to simplification came somewhat later and continued longer. Our study of social studies, literature, grammar, and composition textbooks published between the 1940s and the 1970s (Chall et al., 1977) documents the diminishing difficulty on measures such as readability scores, maturity level, question complexity, and ratio of illustrations to text. Also, as with the decline in difficulty of reading textbooks, some content-area experts questioned the acceleration toward ease, but to little avail. As early as 1937, Ernest Horn, a noted educational researcher and social studies scholar, spoke out against the uncritical, mechanical use of word counts and readability formulas for selecting and rewriting social studies books, since these measures did not adequately consider difficult concepts that students might not understand even though the words used to discuss them might be common (see Chall, 1958). Horn (1937) further predicted that the use of such measures would "not only affect adversely the production, selection and use of books but [would] also result in absurdities that [would] throw research in this field into disrepute" (p. 162).

In sum, the research on text difficulty was extremely effective — perhaps even too effective — in its influence on textbooks. Findings and recommendations from the early studies were readily accepted by teachers, school administrators, and educational publishers. This was despite the fact that most of these studies offered no suggestions for the degree of difficulty that was optimal. Nor did they recommend caution or set limits as to when books might err too far toward ease. Without such knowledge from research and with a growing acceptance by all concerned of the benefits of ease, textbooks became less and less difficult over a period of about half a century.

THE INFLUENCE OF MEASUREMENT INSTRUMENTS

The trend toward ease, as noted earlier, was influenced by the growing availability and use of vocabulary lists and readability formulas. These measurement tools provided an objective evaluation of text and were relatively quick and easy to use. Readability formulas, in particular, became increasingly easy to use as the number of factors needed for reliable prediction was reduced to two (word difficulty or word length and sentence length) and the statistical calculations involved were simplified by tables and graphs and, more recently, by computer programs.

Furthermore, formulas were found to be excellent predictors of difficulty and to be correlated highly with other measures, such as students' scores on comprehension tests and the personal judgments of teachers, librarians, readability experts, and students (Chall, 1958; Chall, Bissex, Conard, & Harris-Sharples, in press; Fry, 1989; Klare, 1963, 1974–1975). Such evidence of their validity, coupled with their objectivity and ease of use, made formulas most attractive to both publishers and school personnel, and their use flourished.

During the past decade, however, the use of these measurement tools, especially formulas, has been questioned. The considerable historical evidence regarding their validity (Fry, 1989) and their propensity to predict difficulty notwithstanding, some have argued that formulas are ineffective as indices of difficulty since they grew from practical needs rather than theoretical constructs (Davison & Green, 1988; Kintsch & Miller, 1984). Another claim is that they do not account for all factors related to difficulty, particularly qualitative ones. Most criticisms, however, have centered on the overzealous use of formulas by publishers and the overreliance of textbook-adoption committees on the books' "scores." The claim is that these misuses have resulted in low-quality writing. By "writing to a formula," publishers have created text that, in general, is choppy, incoherent, and, in its worst state, "primerized," meaning that the written words in no way resemble spoken language. Although publishers are open about their use of formulas, it is difficult to assess accurately the actual extent of "writing to formulas," since the use of selected examples rather than systematic analysis of books is generally the basis on which such inferences are made (see Chapters 5 and 9). What seems to be lost in this exchange is that readability researchers have consistently cautioned against the use of formulas as guides for writing. When they are used in this way, they are used incorrectly.

Another point that is most relevant to any discussion critical of formulas is their connection with simplification in the minds of publishers and educators, which began very shortly after the earliest formulas were developed. Indeed, when these formulas were developed it was usually assumed that greater ease was the goal. In a sense, this outcome could have been predicted, since the early readability and vocabulary studies found textbooks to be too hard for their intended users, and most researchers recommended easier books. Since from their beginnings formulas were widely used by schools to help select books of appropriate difficulty, they quickly became part of the process publishers used to produce books. Had circumstances been different, the use of formulas and word lists could have been associated with the search for and development of challenging textbooks, but it was not until the 1970s that the use of formulas led to such conclusions. Therefore, since word lists and readability formulas were connected with the idea of ease for about half a century, they came to be viewed as instruments for finding and creating easy-to-read texts.

RECENT TRENDS IN THE STUDY OF TEXT DIFFICULTY

In recent years efforts that have benefited the research and theory related to text difficulty have come from a variety of sources.

Some researchers have continued in the conventions of readability measurement and have searched for ways to refine and improve formulas and to make them easier to use. A particular focus here has been on improving the criteria used for developing formulas — from judgment, to multiple-choice comprehension, to cloze tests. Most newer formulas use cloze tests, which correlate highly with text difficulty factors — often .9 or better (Bormuth, 1969; Dale & Chall, in press).

The study of readability has also benefitted from a community of purpose and interest among researchers, resulting in periodic syntheses of the relevant research (Chall, 1958; Klare, 1963, 1974–1975, 1984). Clifford, in her overview of vocabulary research, states that this is quite rare in other areas of reading research.

Another trend has been the assessment of broader, more qualitative aspects of texts. Klare (1984) describes several studies of this type that assess thought units (Lowe, 1979) and phrases (Clark, 1981).

Other researchers have also addressed the qualitative aspects of difficulty by developing assessment scales. These are sets of graded passages that can facilitate judgments of similar text by providing benchmarks for comparison. Of the more recent studies, the Rauding scale (Carver, 1975–1976) and the Holistic Assessment of Texts (Chall et al., in press) cover the broadest range of difficulty, from primary through college level. The SEER (Singer's Eyeball Estimate of Readability) scale (Singer, 1975) is for use with elementary-level text, from first through sixth grade.

These scales differ in the number of passages they include and in their content, but they are similar in that the essential component in their use is judgment and that they rely strongly on judges' experience, insight, and knowledge of language.

Standardization data from these studies indicate that scales are a valid and reliable means of estimating difficulty; evidence shows a reasonably strong correlation with quantitative measures. We see scales as being most valuable for those persons such as teachers and writers who need quick, holistic estimates of difficulty and who rely less on numerical scores. It is interesting that this "new" qualitative tool is in actuality a return to the oldest method of evaluating difficulty: subjective judgment (Chall, 1947).

An especially strong force for the study of text difficulty has come from other disciplines, such as cognitive psychology, linguistics, psycholinguistics, information processing, and artificial intelligence. This focus on difficulty developed in association with the need for greater understanding of how learning occurs and the way in which humans process, store, and recall information.

In contrast to the traditional readability research that studied the linguistic variables of discourse, these newer approaches have turned for insight to the cognitive capabilities of humans. Essentially, the idea underlying all these studies is that there is a structure to thought and memory, as well as to text. The closer the two coincide, the less difficult the text is to read and remember. Relevant to these ideas are Bartlett's (1932) theories of remembering and those of Rumelhart (1980) on schemata. Although the various approaches have much in common, within each of them are specific areas of research interest such as cohesion analysis, story grammar, and propositional analysis.

Research in story grammar or the structure of narrative discourse has demonstrated that narration has an organization or grammar quite similar to the grammar of sentences. One way to conceptualize and explain this organization is in terms of Stein and Glenn's (1979) categories, such as settings, episodes, initiating events, consequences, and so forth. One finding from this research important for the study of difficulty is that stories with clear and easily recognizable grammar are easier to read and remember. Also relevant is the finding that more able and experienced readers make better use of text grammar and understand it better than do the least able or inexperienced readers.

A second area of research — cohesion analysis — has to do with the way a text "fits" together, both at the sentence level and at the text level. Studies in this area have been interested in the overall organization of a book, a chapter, or a paragraph, as well as in the way sentences are related in terms of cohesive ties such as pronouns. The assumption basic to these studies is that more coherent and cohesive text is easier to understand; but, although this idea is intuitively sound, the results of the studies have been mixed (e.g., Freebody & Anderson, 1983; Halliday & Hasan, 1976). Also yet to be answered from this area of study is the level of cohesiveness that most facilitates learning for different levels of reading development, for different individuals, and for different instructional purposes.

A third related area of research — propositional analysis — has produced promising results for understanding and predicting difficulty. In propositional analysis, a text is analyzed into basic units of meaning that are then used to build a structure of text which is enlarged or changed in some way with the addition of each proposition. The work of Kintsch and his associates (e.g., Kintsch & Vipond, 1979; Miller & Kintsch, 1980) and Meyer (1977, 1984) has suggested the value of this approach as part of our analysis of textbooks. However, our trial applications of propositional analysis as well as measures of cohesion indicated that they were still too complex and detailed for the analysis we were planning for more than seventy textbooks.

Therefore, in addition to readability formulas, we used several broad, cognitive measures to enlarge and deepen our analysis: for example, reading stages; a measure of question complexity (factual to inferential); the attention given to meaning vocabulary, reading comprehension, study skills, and writing; and the extent and kinds of illustrations used.

STANDARDS FOR TEXT DIFFICULTY

Another caution often disregarded in discussions of formulas and their use is that readability scores tell how hard a text is, not how hard it should be. Optimal difficulty—for learning to read, for comprehending subject-matter textbooks, and for the advancement of reading—depends upon many other factors besides the readability score, for example, the reading abilities, interests, and background of the readers; the kind of learning expected; and the assistance received from a teacher or a more knowledge-able peer.

Some insight into potential standards for optimal difficulty can be found in the procedures used to standardize formulas. For example, in most readability studies, the most common criterion used to establish the difficulty of text passages is a measure of reading comprehension, generally the ability of students within a certain grade to answer correctly about 75% of a set of multiple-choice questions, usually about main ideas, details, and inferences. According to Bormuth (1975), this figure is a slight alteration of an 80% accuracy criterion introduced by Thorndike (1916) early in his research, designed to represent an "adequate" level of comprehension. Thus, a fifth-grade readability score for a given book means that the average student in fifth grade would be able to answer at least 75% of questions asked, all other things being equal.

When formula scores are used to select textbooks, the rule of thumb has been to choose a book with a readability score that is consistent with the reading grade equivalent of students on a standardized reading test.

While the figure used is often the average for an entire class, the wide variations in reading ability in most classes make the choice of a single book quite difficult. A single class may span as many as five to seven grade levels, and different students may be able to read different content materials at different levels.

Through the years, few have questioned the use of a single score for different instructional purposes, although the widely used Informal Reading Inventory (Betts, 1946) provides different word recognition and comprehension criteria for instructional and independent reading. A model for identifying different difficulty criteria for different reading purposes was developed by Bormuth in 1971. Although this model has not been widely replicated, a readability formula developed from Bormuth's research was the basis for the Degrees of Reading Power (DRP), a test used to assess both students' reading abilities and the readability of the text (College Entrance Examination Board, 1980).

Concerns about the use of readability formula scores as exact measures rather than as estimates of difficulty have also been rare until just recently. Yet researchers have consistently found that, when more than one formula is applied to the same book, the results may vary by two or more grade levels. Such discrepancies are related to differences in sampling, the different predictive powers of the formulas, and the different text factors assessed by them (Chall, 1958; Conard, 1984; Klare, 1963). They are a strong reminder that formulas must be used with care and understanding.

Further insights into effective ways of setting standards for instructional programs and materials are available from cognitive and developmental theories. Although their influence in this area has been indirect and thus far weaker than the empirical research, cognitive and developmental theories are gaining importance. Primary among them are those of Piaget (1936/1952, 1964, 1968), Vygotsky (1962, 1978), Bruner (1960, 1966), Carroll (1963), and Bloom (1964, 1976). We will be concerned here with ideas that relate to optimal difficulty and challenge for reading and learning.

Overall, all these theories are concerned with the match between a learner's entering abilities and the difficulty of the instructional task, which includes the materials used. The difficulty of the task is seen as affecting not only how much is learned, but also the onset of the next stage of development. If the match is optimal, learning is enhanced and the learner's growth is encouraged and accelerated. If the match is not optimal, learning is less efficient and development may be halted. A student's self-concept may also be negatively affected by a poor match.

In their writings, all these authorities — with the possible exception of Piaget — clearly define an optimal match as being slightly above the learner's current level of functioning. That is, they believe that learning and instruction should somewhat precede development. Interpretations of Piaget's position call for instruction either slightly ahead of development (McNally, 1973) or at least consistent with it (Sullivan, 1967). In none of the theories is it recommended that learning be on a level lower than that of development.

The strongest argument for task difficulty beyond that of development is found in Vygotsky's (1962, 1978) writings. He emphasizes that optimal difficulty is influenced by the amount of instruction given during learning. The greater the amount of instruction, the more difficult the task can be. The area of difference in the difficulty between what a learner can accomplish independently, without instruction, and what can be learned with instruction Vygotsky calls the "zone of proximal development" (1978, p. 86).

These theorists also consider the question of individual differences as well as of general developmental differences, in defining optimal learning and instruction. Although they offer no clear guidelines for accommodating individual differences, they imply that different difficulty levels may be optimal for particular levels of development or according to differences in abilities. Exemplifying this position is Vygotsky's (1978) statement that the relationship between developmental and learning processes is highly complex and cannot be encompassed by an unchanging hypothetical formulation.

CONCLUSION

The research on the theory and measurement of text difficulty has a long history. It has resulted in useful knowledge and tools which, overall, have been constructive in the development, selection, and use of textbooks and other instructional materials. As in other areas of education and human endeavor, however, there have been misunderstandings and misuses of these ideas and instruments. It would seem unfortunate if this accumulation of knowledge and the tools developed from it were ignored. If we walk away from the empirical research on difficulty, it might well be that we will have to rediscover it. Indeed, the theoretical position of Vygotsky on optimal difficulty seems to be more compelling to many researchers than the similar empirical evidence on reading difficulty.

CHAPTER 3

Publishers' Views About Suitable Reading Level

At one time, textbooks for elementary and secondary classrooms were known by the names of their authors. Among those that have become part of our heritage are Webster's Blue Back Spellers, McGuffey's Readers, and Muzzy's American history books. In recent years textbooks have become better known by the names of their publishers (the Ginn Readers, Heath Science) since, rather than being the work of an individual, they are written by panels of authors, advisors, and consultants for publishing and development houses. Thus, in order to gain insights into how decisions are made about text difficulty (or what we will refer to here as "suitable reading level"), we went first to the leading textbook publishers.

We wanted to discover what publishers think about this issue. Is a suitable level of reading difficulty for each grade important to them, even though some researchers have argued that such concern is unwarranted (Armbruster, Osborn, & Davison, 1985)? To explore their views, we surveyed editors and administrators who develop elementary and secondary textbooks. Eighty-four individuals representing 34 publishing companies responded to our mailed questionnaire and provided us with information and insights on the importance placed on suitable reading level and how they decided what level was optimal. (Appendix A–1 presents a list of educational publishing houses participating in the surveys, while Appendix A–2 provides a copy of the questionnaire sent to publishers of secondary textbooks.)

IMPORTANCE OF SUITABLE READING LEVEL

To most of the publishers who participated in the survey, suitable reading level was an important consideration. As shown in Table 3.1, almost two-thirds rated it as more important than publishing costs, the

TABLE 3.1: Percentage of Publishers Rating Suitable Reading Level More Important Than Other Publishing Concerns

"Suitable reading level is more or much more important than":	Percentage of Publishers		
	Elementary $(n = 73)$	Secondary $(n = 11)$	All $(N = 84)$
Physical features: design and graphics	65	50	63
Publication cost	58	82	61
Personnel: authors and editors	59	73	61
Teacher's manuals	44	64	46
Treatment of "sensitive" issues			
Race, sex, ethnic groups	36	18	33
Topics such as evolution, reproduction	44	9	39
Content	22	18	21
Organization of chapters, sections, etc.	55	27	51

physical aspects of a book, and decisions about personnel. There were, however, some aspects of textbooks that the majority of publishers thought more important than reading level. These were related to content and such sensitive issues as minority representation and the treatment of controversial topics.

Some interesting differences were found in responses that were associated with whether the respondents worked with elementary or secondary textbooks. For example, publishers of secondary textbooks were more concerned about the way a book was organized and illustrated and the way in which sensitive issues were treated. Publishers of elementary textbooks were also more concerned with content and the treatment of minority groups, but they were more concerned than secondary teachers about effective manuals.

These differences seem to corroborate certain other research. Censorship of textbooks, for example, has been found more frequently at higher than at lower grades (Kamhi, 1981), and the topics most often targeted for censorship—reproduction and evolution—are commonly studied in high school (Chall & Conard, 1984). Hence, the treatment of sensitive issues would more likely be an overall concern for the publishers of secondary than elementary textbooks.

Our observations of the way textbooks are used in secondary science and social studies classes (to be discussed in Chapter 7) also support secondary publishers' concerns with organization of books and graphics. At the secondary level, textbooks are more often assigned for independent study, without a lot of introduction by teachers; explicit presentation and clear organization are more important for independent learning. Furthermore, vocabulary and concepts have a stronger correlation with reading difficulty at lower levels, whereas at higher levels the relationship between ideas — the organization — takes on greater importance.

The elementary textbook publishers' stronger ratings on the importance of teacher's manuals are also consistent with both practice and research (Chall, 1967; Durkin, 1984; see also Chapter 6). Teacher's manuals are particularly important in basal reading programs, which constitute the largest part of elementary school budgets for instructional materials (Chall & Squire, 1991).

Thus the publishers' self-reports about the importance of suitable reading level gain in reliability from the differences found between publishers responsible for elementary or secondary books. Comments added by many publishers also reinforced their responses. For example, one remarked, "Reading level is of prime importance to customers. It is invariably the first question that is asked." Its importance relative to other factors was noted by another: "A level of suitable difficulty is an integral part of all items mentioned; it is just one part of putting together a quality program."

ASSESSMENT OF SUITABLE READING LEVEL

Let us now look at our findings on how publishers assess difficulty. Our survey measured their reliance on both objective techniques and on subjective judgments.

As can be seen in Table 3.2, almost all publishers said they used quantitative devices to assess the difficulty of their books. They compared the text with various vocabulary lists and applied readability formulas. Most secondary publishers also evaluated the difficulty and density of concepts, while very few elementary publishers confirmed that they did.

Publishers also said they relied strongly on judgment — their own and that of others. The publishers of elementary books said they most frequently sought the views of authors and editors and of school personnel. The publishers of secondary books relied the most on the advice of specialists and consultants. More than half of the publishers confirmed that they sought the advice of their marketing departments, although this group was the least often mentioned.

Thus it seems that quantitative techniques — formulas and word lists — form the main basis for publishers' assessment of suitable reading level. But publishers also rely quite extensively on subjective evaluations, seeking advice primarily from school people, their own authors and editors, special consultants and experts, and their marketing departments.

We also asked whether, prior to publication of textbooks, publishers tested them on a student population. Only a few reported that they did; of

TABLE 3.2:   How Publishers Evaluate Suitable Reading Level

	Percentage of Publishers*		
Evaluation criterion	Elementary $(n = 73)$	Secondary $(n = 11)$	All $(N = 84)$
What methods are used?			
Vocabulary lists	100	91	99
Readability formulas	89	100	90
Measures of concepts	17	91	28
Whose judgments are used?			
Authors' and editors'	93	82	92
School personnel's	94	73	92
Specialists' and consultants'	62	91	65
Marketing personnel's	56	55	56

*The percentages include those who gave ratings of either "often" or "always."

these, most did not respond to our questions on how such testing was conducted.

DEFINING SUITABLE READING LEVEL

We sought also to determine how publishers define a suitable reading level and whether their definition is influenced by the subject of a textbook or the ability of students who use it.

To find out how they define suitable reading level, we asked elementary publishers whether science and social studies books should be easier than, equal in difficulty to, or harder than reading textbooks. (Secondary publishers were not asked this question, since reading textbooks are not generally used in high schools.) As shown in Table 3.3, most elementary publishers said science and social studies books should be equal in difficulty to or easier than reading textbooks. No more than 15% thought social studies or science textbooks should be harder. But, as one publisher expressed it, "Reading levels in science and social studies books will necessarily be higher because of the increased frequency of more difficult terms." As we shall see in Chapter 5, this statement describes a persisting dilemma.

With regard to publishers' views of suitable reading level relative to the current reading abilities of students, publishers of both elementary and secondary textbooks generally agreed that, for students of above-average reading ability, textbooks should be at least somewhat above their achievement levels (see Table 3.4). For students of average reading ability, more tended to think that textbooks should be about equal to student reading achievement, although many still thought they should be higher. The pub-

TABLE 3.3: **Elementary Publishers' Views of Suitable Reading Level for Science and Social Studies Books (*N* = 69)**

	Percentage of Elementary Publishers	
"Compared to reading textbooks for the same grade, science and social studies textbooks should be":	Science Textbooks	Social Studies Textbooks
Much more or somewhat more difficult	15	13
Of the same difficulty level	42	49
Much less or somewhat less difficult	43	37

lishers differed, however, in their views of suitable reading level for students reading below grade level. A majority of secondary publishers thought the textbooks for these students should be equal to their reading achievement level, while elementary publishers were more evenly divided among the options, with the highest number — 38 % — saying that such students should use books below their reading level.

SUMMARY OF SURVEY RESULTS

Our survey indicated that publishers rated suitable reading level as central in the development of both elementary and high school textbooks. They saw this factor as more important than cost, choice of personnel, and the physical features of books. It was rated less important than content and the treatment of such issues as ethnic and minority representation and topics of a sensitive nature.

Publishers reported using readability formulas and vocabulary lists as measures of reading level, and also reported relying on their subjective

TABLE 3.4: **Publishers' Views of Suitable Reading Level for Different Levels of Student Reading Achievement**

	Percentage of Publishers Preferring Textbook Reading Level Difficulty		
Student Reading Achievement Level	Somewhat or Much Higher	The Same	Somewhat or Much Lower
ELEMENTARY STUDENTS			
Above average (*n* = 63)	84	14	2
Average (*n* = 60)	48	45	7
Below average (*n* = 56)	30	32	38
SECONDARY STUDENTS			
Above average (*n* = 11)	82	18	0
Average (*n* = 10)	40	60	0
Below average (*n* = 11)	18	55	27

judgments and on the judgments of school personnel, subject-matter experts, and those responsible for marketing. Field testing on a student population was reported only by a few publishers, and still fewer reported on how it was done. A reasonable explanation for the paucity of responses on field tests may be the proprietary nature of these practices and the strong competitiveness among publishers that prohibits sharing of information viewed as confidential (Squire, 1988).

Publishers' ideas about suitable reading level were influenced both by the books' content — social studies and science as compared to reading — and by student reading achievement levels.

At least 85% of the elementary publishers said social studies and science books should be no more difficult than reading books. Yet many of them mentioned that content textbooks might actually be more difficult, since their purpose differed from that of reading textbooks and the concepts they included were likely to be unfamiliar. In Chapter 5, our textbook analyses indicate that higher difficulty in content textbooks is, indeed, a fact. So, while content does affect ideas about suitable difficulty, the reality may differ from what publishers prefer, or from what they think teachers prefer.

We also found publishers' views of suitable reading level to be influenced by students' reading achievement levels. Overall, higher challenge was the preference for students reading above average, moderate challenge for average students, and lesser challenge for those reading below average. Differences found between elementary and secondary publishers' preferences according to reading ability may be related to the actual difficulty of books for higher or lower grades, in relation to the reading levels of students. For example, we found high school textbooks to be relatively easier for the grades for which they are intended (see Chapter 5) and also easier according to students' tested comprehension and their subjective judgments of difficulty (see Chapter 8). Such findings also correspond to those we reported in our earlier comparison (Chall et al., 1977) of textbooks and SAT scores: Eleventh-grade social studies textbooks were relatively easier in relation to students' reading achievement than those published for lower grades.

REVIEW OF THE LITERATURE: 1985–1989

The great concern that we found among publishers for the suitable reading level of textbooks, as well as their preference for using objective means to evaluate this factor, seemed to us to be counter to much of the current professional writing on textbooks. To test this idea, we reviewed a sample of recent articles and books written about textbooks and level of difficulty. Publication dates of the 12 articles and books were from 1985 to 1989 (see Appendix B-3).

Essentially, the common theme of these professional articles was that the difficulty level of textbooks was an unimportant issue. Furthermore, most claimed that the use of readability formulas and word lists was responsible for the low quality of writing; publishers used them to write or rewrite books to prescribed "grade levels."

Since our surveys of publishers reported in this chapter were conducted in the early 1980s, before the wide questioning of the use of quantitative measurement tools, we wondered if we could find any evidence that publishers were indeed less concerned with suitable level of difficulty in the late 1980s as compared to the early 1980s.

For insight concerning changes in publishers' views, we compared their discussions of difficulty in the teacher's manuals of the early 1980s with the manuals of the late 1980s. Second, we compared the difficulty of the books published in the early 1980s with the difficulty of those published in the late 1980s. We present here only a few highlights. (See Chapters 5 and 6 for the full findings.)

From the teacher's manuals, we learned that publishers are still strongly concerned with appropriate difficulty of texts. However, the way they discuss difficulty seems changed. Instead of writing about the readability of their books, many publishers use the words *learnability* or *teachability*, terms that seem synonomous with readability but perhaps more acceptable in an atmosphere that has become increasingly skeptical toward readability measurement. Yet in spite of this reluctance, we found the readability score of textbooks for the same grade published in the late 1970s and the late 1980s to be remarkably similar. These comparisons are reported in detail in Chapter 5.

CHAPTER 4

Teachers' Views About Suitable Reading Level

To gain a better understanding of educators' views on textbook difficulty in the schools, we conducted a nationwide mailed survey and a series of intensive interviews of teachers. Two hundred twenty-seven teachers and curriculum specialists responded to the survey, and follow-up interviews were conducted with teachers in the classrooms we observed. The elementary schools we studied included kindergarten through eighth grade. We therefore report the data for eighth-grade classes with our elementary-level findings, mindful that the eighth grade may also be found in middle and junior high schools. (The questionnaire sent to secondary teachers is reproduced in Appendix A–3.)

Many of the questions asked of teachers paralleled those asked of publishers, as discussed in Chapter 3. We asked about the relative importance of suitable reading level in selecting a textbook and how such an evaluation was made. We asked teachers what level of difficulty they considered optimal for students with various levels of reading achievement, as well as for use with individuals, or with smaller and larger groups. Our interviews were designed to elaborate on and to confirm or disconfirm the responses from the survey.

IMPORTANCE OF SUITABLE READING LEVEL

Similar to the responses from publishers, all teachers, whether they taught in elementary or high school, said the suitable reading level of a book was clearly a primary consideration for them in the selection process (see Table 4.1). Elementary teachers, especially, viewed suitable reading level as vitally important: Approximately three-quarters of them gave it a higher priority than all other considerations except one — content and con-

TABLE 4.1: Percentage of Surveyed Teachers Rating Suitable Reading Level Higher Than Other Selection Concerns

"Suitable reading level is more or much more important than":	Percentage of Teachers		
	Elementary (*n* = 182)	Secondary (*n* = 45)	All (*N* = 225)
Physical features: design and graphics	79	78	78
Cost: initial price and durability	77	82	78
Teaching aids: supplementary materials and tests	85	73	82
Teacher's manuals	79	71	77
Alignment with curriculum and learning objectives	70	62	68
Evidence of pretesting	76	76	76
Treatment of race, sex, ethnic groups	71	51	67
Content and concepts	59	38	55
Organization of chapters, sections, etc.	73	47	67

cepts. Even for this factor, suitable level maintained its advantage in over half of the responses.

Secondary teachers also considered suitable reading level of prime importance in almost all comparisons. More than elementary teachers, however, teachers in high schools were about equally concerned with reading level and the treatment given to sensitive issues such as race, sex, and ethnic groups; and the way books were organized. Further, only about one-third of high school teachers rated content and concepts as more important than suitable reading level.

The high priority that teachers placed on reading level is underscored by comments that many included on their questionnaires. Some simply said that it was of "utmost importance" or a "top priority." Others wrote more extensively of the impossibility of considering any other aspect above that of reading level. "Without a suitable level of difficulty, what importance do these other items have?" "Unless a text is written at an appropriate difficulty level, what difference does it make if it is up to date with beautiful illustrations?"

The results of the interviews confirmed the findings from the teachers' survey: About two-thirds of those interviewed said suitable reading level was a major consideration. Their comments further suggested that it was particularly important for students in the higher rather than lower grades and for content books, such as texts in science and social studies, rather than for reading textbooks. An eighth-grade teacher described his students as "generally less enthusiastic" than younger ones and "therefore books of appropriate difficulty are more important for them." Another commented, "The difficulty level of the book 'colors' the student's attitude toward the content of a subject. . . . Students do not like books that are too hard to understand, nor do they like books that are so easy they don't learn new ideas."

Also consistent with survey results were the findings from the interviews on the greater importance placed on content and concepts. A fourth-grade teacher who did not use textbooks in his science class said he made this decision because none of the books were suitable in "depth of treatment" of any topic. A sixth-grade science teacher described students as "able to decode words, but unable to understand concepts such as 'molecules,' 'sound waves,' 'fission,' 'fusion,' 'mass,' and 'energy.' . . . Such words can be read by elementary and junior high school students, but they represent concepts that are difficult for them to grasp." Representing the thoughts of several others was an eighth-grade teacher's wish that publishers would produce books with sophisticated ideas but on lower reading levels.

ASSESSMENT OF SUITABLE READING LEVEL

Teachers' responses to our questions regarding how they assessed reading level were similar to those of publishers. As can be seen in Table 4.2, teachers frequently used quantitative techniques, although not as extensively as publishers (compare Table 3.2). Vocabulary lists were used frequently by over half of all the teachers surveyed, but by more elementary than high school teachers. Readability formulas were relied upon by similarly large percentages of elementary and secondary teachers.

Even more often than they used formulas or word lists, teachers said

TABLE 4.2: How Surveyed Teachers Evaluate Suitable Reading Level

	Percentage of Teachers*		
Evaluation criterion	Elementary $(n = 180)$	Secondary $(n = 45)$	All $(N = 225)$
WHAT METHODS ARE USED?			
Vocabulary lists	62	51	60
Readability formulas	61	62	61
Measures of concepts	86	81	85
Student tests or try-outs	67	32	60
WHOSE JUDGMENTS ARE USED?			
One's own	90	93	91
Publisher's assigned readability levels	76	53	72
Co-workers'	72	71	72
Supervisor's and Principal's	61	48	59
Students'	46	33	43

they evaluated the conceptual difficulty of textbooks. Our impression is that such evaluations were generally qualitative, since measures of conceptual difficulty are still primarily in the research stage. [See, for example, Flesch's (1950) measure of the level of abstraction, Morriss and Holversen's (1935) idea analysis technique, and Kemper's (1983) inference load measurement.]

Testing books with students was a technique reported much more often by teachers than publishers. Over twice as many elementary as secondary teachers reported the frequent use of this method.

Judgment played a large part in teachers' assessments of reading level. Almost three-quarters of the teachers said they asked other teachers about a book's level, to confirm their own impression. Elementary teachers were more likely to use the readability level assigned by publishers than were high school teachers. They were also more likely to enlist the help of supervisory personnel and students.

The teachers we interviewed reported similar frequency of use of these as did survey respondents. Vocabulary lists, readability formulas, and conceptual measures were mentioned most frequently. The readability level assigned to books by publishers was used primarily for elementary reading textbooks, not for subject-matter textbooks.

DETERMINING SUITABLE READING LEVEL

Type of Textbook

Elementary teachers were asked how difficult they thought their content textbooks should be in relation to the difficulty of their reading textbooks. This question was asked only of elementary classroom teachers, since they teach all these subjects. Their responses are shown in Table 4.3.

Most elementary teachers said the social studies and science books should be at the same level or easier than the reading books. Only 16%

TABLE 4.3: Surveyed Elementary Teachers' Views of Suitable Reading Level for Science and Social Studies Books ($N = 182$)

	Percentage of Elementary Teachers	
"Compared to reading textbooks for the same grade, science and social studies textbooks should be":	Science Textbooks	Social Studies Textbooks
Much more or somewhat more difficult	16	16
Of the same difficulty level	44	45
Much less or somewhat less difficult	41	39

preferred higher levels of difficulty for the content textbooks than for reading books used in the same grade. These responses were almost identical to those of the elementary publishers (refer to Table 3.3). There was also great similarity in teachers' and publishers' awareness that elementary-level content textbooks are generally harder than reading books. Such a view is summarized quite succinctly by one teacher's statement that "reading levels in science and social studies books will necessarily be harder because of the increased frequency of more difficult terms." But many teachers said the content books were so difficult that they became a real "source of frustration," so, whenever it was possible, they made a point to select "easier ones, since only one book per grade could be chosen." Comments of other teachers suggested that, while they agreed that content textbooks were usually harder than reading textbooks and needed to be harder in order to teach new concepts, adjustments needed to be made in their use. For example, one teacher mentioned "reading all the necessary information to her class," while another said she "did a lot orally — discussing and explaining."

Our analyses of science and social studies textbooks (see Chapter 5) show that teachers are quite accurate in their assessments of the difficulty of these books. In almost all instances, the content textbooks were substantially more difficult than the reading textbooks for the same grades, particularly in the fourth grade. Perhaps such reality motivates elementary teachers to say they prefer content books that are easier than they actually are, that is, either equal to or less difficult than reading textbooks.

Level of Student Reading Achievement

We also explored whether teachers' views of suitable reading level were influenced by their students' level of reading achievement. We asked whether they preferred easier or harder textbooks in relation to the reading ability of their average, above-average, and below-average readers. The results are shown in Table 4.4.

Over three-quarters of both elementary- and secondary-survey respondents said that above-average readers should be challenged by their textbooks; therefore, the difficulty of their books should be above their reading level. A majority of teachers also said that average students should use books above their reading level. But for below-average readers, about half said the same level of difficulty would be most suitable, and 37% of elementary teachers preferred an even lower difficulty level.

Findings from our interviews of elementary teachers confirmed those from the survey. For above-average readers, most teachers of fourth-, sixth-, and eighth-grade classes preferred more challenging texts, that is, texts

TABLE 4.4: Surveyed Teachers' Views of Suitable Reading Level for Different Levels of Student Reading Achievement

Student Reading Achievement Level	Percentage of Teachers Preferring Textbook Reading Level Difficulty		
	Somewhat or Much Higher	The Same	Somewhat or Much Lower
ELEMENTARY STUDENTS			
Above average ($n = 168$)	77	20	3
Average ($n = 162$)	52	36	12
Below average ($n = 150$)	21	42	37
SECONDARY STUDENTS			
Above average ($n = 45$)	87	11	2
Average ($n = 45$)	59	36	4
Below average ($n = 45$)	32	55	14

above the students' reading levels (see Table 4.5). Generally, the higher the grade taught, the greater the preference for challenging texts. The predominant theme was that good readers work well when challenged. The preference for challenging books for higher achievers was consistent for all three subjects — reading, science, and social studies.

For average readers, half of the fourth-grade teachers preferred textbooks at the same level of difficulty as the students' reading ability. Accompanying this preference was the explanation that, when text difficulty and student reading achievement matched, a more "comfortable" reading ex-

TABLE 4.5: Interviewed Elementary Teachers' Views of Suitable Reading Level for Different Levels of Student Reading Achievement

STUDENT READING ACHIEVEMENT LEVEL/Grade	Percentage of Teachers Preferring Textbook Reading Level Difficulty		
	Higher	The Same	Lower
ABOVE AVERAGE			
Fourth grade ($n = 17$)	76	18	6
Sixth grade ($n = 22$)	82	18	0
Eighth grade ($n = 27$)	97	4	0
AVERAGE			
Fourth grade ($n = 18$)	39	50	11
Sixth grade ($n = 24$)	58	42	0
Eighth grade ($n = 27$)	71	26	4
BELOW AVERAGE			
Fourth grade ($n = 18$)	39	39	23
Sixth grade ($n = 22$)	14	32	54
Eighth grade ($n = 27$)	26	33	41

perience is effected. But over half of sixth-grade teachers and nearly three-quarters of eighth-grade teachers preferred higher levels of difficulty for these average readers. They contended that more challenging textbooks presented not only *more* content, but *more interesting* content. These teachers also noted the positive effects of more difficult materials on students' comprehension and on the quantity and quality of their work.

Teachers' interview responses to the question of suitable reading levels for their average students varied somewhat according to the subject they taught. For reading and social studies, more teachers of all grades preferred books above these students' reading levels. But for science, more preferred books equal to their reading levels.

For below-average readers, sixth- and eighth-grade teachers preferred a level of difficulty equal to or below student reading achievement, whereas fourth-grade teachers preferred difficulty equal to or above. For this level there were also some differences according to the subjects teachers taught. For reading, they tended to prefer more difficult textbooks for below-average readers than they did for either science or social studies. For science and social studies, teachers spoke of the need for easier books for these students to "build up their self-confidence."

From both the survey and interviews, one trend is evident: Conceptions of challenge are related to the level of students' achievement. For students of above-average and average achievement, more is expected in relation to what they are currently able to do. For students of below-average reading achievement, less is expected. Most of the teachers' comments regarding books for these readers reflected affective concerns about their students' emotional well-being. They suggested that below-average readers are "more easily frustrated" and "feel more secure if their reading is done well." Thus, the teachers said they preferred textbooks with less challenge relative to reading ability. Only a few teachers indicated that challenge may benefit below-average readers as well. One teacher commented, "Even for lower students, if the book is too easy, where is the feeling of accomplishment?"

Group Size, Grade, and Subject

Teachers were also asked about the influence of group size on their preferences for difficulty. Did teaching larger or smaller groups make a difference? Elementary teachers' responses, shown in Table 4.6, indicate that irrespective of the size of the group or the subject being taught, a clear majority said they preferred a reading level matched to the average reading ability of their students.

When working with larger groups of students or classes (12 or more),

TABLE 4.6:   Surveyed Elementary Teachers' Views of Suitable Reading Level for Different Size Groups

SIZE OF INSTRUCTIONAL GROUP/Subject	"Reading level should be matched to the reading ability of":		
	Above-Average Readers	Average Readers	Below-Average Readers
20 OR MORE STUDENTS			
Reading (*n* = 175)	8	83	9
Science (*n* = 173)	7	70	22
Social Studies (*n* = 172)	8	74	18
10 TO 19 STUDENTS			
Reading (*n* = 177)	11	81	7
Science (*n* = 172)	9	84	7
Social Studies (*n* = 172)	9	76	16
2 TO 9 STUDENTS			
Reading (*n* = 171)	22	66	12
Science (*n* = 173)	14	67	19
Social Studies (*n* = 175)	15	69	15

secondary level teachers also preferred a reading level suitable for average students, as shown in Table 4.7. When selecting books for fewer students (2 to 9), however, about equal numbers of secondary teachers preferred to match to the average and above-average readers. Thus it seems that high school teachers' decisions about reading level may be more influenced by group size — the smaller the group, the harder the book can be.

Interviews with elementary and secondary teachers confirm the survey finding that teachers in higher grades are more apt to be influenced by group size. Table 4.8 shows that one-half or more of the fourth- and sixth-grade teachers prefer to match the textbook reading level to the reading

TABLE 4.7:   Surveyed Secondary Teachers' and Publishers' Views of Suitable Reading Level for Different Size Groups

RESPONDENTS/Size of Instructional Group	"Reading level should be matched to the reading ability of":		
	Above-Average Readers	Average Readers	Below-Average Readers
TEACHERS			
20 or more students (*n* = 45)	7	84	9
10 to 19 students (*n* = 45)	16	82	2
2 to 9 students (*n* = 45)	47	47	7
PUBLISHERS			
20 or more students (*n* = 10)	0	100	0
10 to 19 students (*n* = 11)	9	91	0
2 to 9 students (*n* = 11)	9	91	0

TABLE 4.8: Interviewed Teachers' Views of Suitable Reading Level for Their Classes

| Grade level of teacher | Textbook Reading Level Compared to Average Student Reading Ability | | |
	Somewhat or Much Higher	The Same	Somewhat or Much Lower
Fourth-grade teachers ($n = 18$)	12	61	28
Sixth-grade teachers ($n = 14$)	43	50	7
Eighth-grade teachers ($n = 8$)	75	25	0
Eleventh-grade			
Social Studies teachers ($n = 9$)	55	33	11
Science teachers ($n = 9$)	55	44	0

abilities of average students, whereas over one-half or more of the eighth- and eleventh-grade teachers prefer a higher reading level.

This question was not included in the elementary publishers' survey, but secondary publishers were asked to indicate the reading level of books they would recommend to teachers for different group sizes. Their recommendations (see Table 4.7, above) are for a reading level matched to the average students regardless of group size.

COMPARISON OF TEACHERS' AND PUBLISHERS' RESPONSES

We can now compare the views on difficulty expressed by publishers, who produce textbooks, and teachers, who purchase and use them. Teachers' responses to the question of suitable reading level for students of different reading achievement levels (Table 4.4) were quite consistent with those of publishers (Table 3.4). In fact, all questions asked of both publishers and teachers revealed essentially similar results. Both groups considered suitable reading level to be very important and used objective and qualitative measures as the means for evaluating it. Readability formulas and word lists were the objective methods used most often and, of qualitative measures, evaluations of conceptual difficulty were used frequently by most teachers and by secondary publishers, but infrequently by elementary publishers.

One-third of secondary teachers and two-thirds of elementary teachers mentioned testing a book's difficulty with students. Few of the publishers we surveyed confirmed testing their books on prospective students, although other sources say this is almost always done (Squire, 1988).

Overall, both publishers and teachers expressed similar views on suitable reading level of books for different subjects and different student reading achievement levels. This strong similarity may be an indication that publishers are indeed aware of teachers' views and model their products to fit them. In general, teachers' preferences for suitable reading level seem to be influenced by classroom characteristics such as grade level and subject taught; in the case of secondary teachers, the size of the group also exerts an influence. Publishers' preferences seem most affected by the content of the book and are less influenced by other classroom variables than teachers' preferences are.

AN UPDATE ON TEACHERS' VIEWS

The survey and interviews reported in this chapter were conducted in the early 1980s, before much of the current strong criticism of textbooks. To see what might have changed, we took a look at a more recent survey of teachers by Rogers (1988), for a comparison and update. Rogers questioned 100 elementary and secondary teachers and conducted six follow-up interviews. From a review of 30 current critical publications on textbooks, he developed a questionnaire based on five categories: readability, content, organization, controversial issues, and "general" criticisms. His purpose was to find whether teachers agreed with recent criticisms of textbooks. The findings were published on the commentary page of the widely read *Education Week* on August 3, 1988.

Rogers (1988) found the majority of the teachers surveyed disagreed with much of the current criticism of textbooks. They agreed primarily with criticisms unrelated to the textbooks themselves, but directed to such aspects as how they are selected. For example, most agreed that the textbook-adoption process needs improvement and that teachers should play a major role in it. Most disagreed with textbook critics that the quality of textbooks has been "declining drastically" during the past 10 years, or that textbooks are "flat," "unimaginative," written in a "choppy and stilted" style, "lacking in continuity," and saturated with "pointless workbook exercises."

With regard to suitable reading level, it is significant to note that Rogers's (1988) findings are essentially the same as those we found in the early 1980s. "Appropriate readability levels characterize good textbooks for these teachers, as does the inclusion of guidelines to help them adopt the books for use with students of varying abilities and needs" (Rogers, 1988, p. 56).

In general, the teachers Rogers (1988) surveyed, as compared to most critics today, gave textbooks a high rating, mentioning only that they could be improved by an increase in attention to thinking skills. The teachers also said that, in contrast to earlier books, the more recently published books are better in most respects.

The reaction to Rogers's (1988) report was swift. Within a few weeks, several responses appeared in the letters column of *Education Week* (1988). One applauded and concurred with his findings, while others disagreed strongly, questioning his methodology in general and the teachers' ability to judge textbooks in particular. One, in fact, said simply that teachers are poor judges of textbooks and therefore their views are of limited importance. Such quick critical outcries suggest that textbooks will, for some time to come, remain a topic of considerable controversy.

CHAPTER 5

A Comparative Analysis of Content Textbooks

In this chapter we look to textbooks themselves for evidence about difficulty. We analyzed them to see how difficult they actually were and whether they offered a range of reading levels appropriate for the wide differences in the abilities of students in each grade. We also looked to see if the difficulty of books had changed over a 15-year period in ways that might reflect the many calls made during that time for more demanding and rigorous books.

We chose to analyze content textbooks since, above the first few grades, these books provide the primary vehicle for students' learning from text as well as for the development of their reading skills. In addition, content textbooks have been a particular target of much of the recent criticism (e.g., Anderson & Armbruster, 1984; FitzGerald, 1979). Two content areas were represented in our sample — science and social studies — and the books were for both elementary and high school — Grades 4, 8, and 11. To obtain as representative a sample as possible, we asked publishers to supply books in three categories: those intended to be widely used, those for above-average readers, and those for below-average readers. Two collections of books were analyzed: Sample one included those published between 1974 and 1982 (the majority of books were published from 1979 to 1982), and sample two contained those published between 1985 and 1989. The first sample was larger (46 books) and was analyzed more extensively. The second sample (21 books) was identified by educational publishers as containing the most popular books for the three grades we surveyed. It provided a basis for comparison and evidence of stability or change. (A complete listing of the books used in this analysis is given in Appendix B–1.)

To provide a comprehensive perspective on the difficulty of the 1974–1982 collection of books, we used a variety of indicators: readability level, the complexity of questions asked, the extent and kinds of illustrations, and an estimate of overall cognitive demands. To measure readability, we used the Dale-Chall readability formula (Dale & Chall, 1948). For evaluating question complexity, we used a modification of the taxonomy developed by Bloom (1956), which is explained in Appendix D–1. Questions in the textbooks and accompanying workbooks were analyzed, but, since questions in both were so similar, we report only those in the textbooks. Illustrations were analyzed according to categories of frequency, type, and purpose. The maturity or cognitive level of the books was assessed by estimating the stage of reading development required to read and comprehend a sample of text. This criterion is derived from the model of reading development developed by Chall (1983b) and is presented in Appendix D–2.

There were no precedents to use for studying the effects of illustrations on reading difficulty, although it is generally accepted that illustrations contribute to the comprehension of text. Since illustrations play a large role in content textbooks, we analyzed our sample of books in terms of the amount and kinds of illustrations presented to determine whether they were related in some way to the grade placement, linguistic difficulty, content, or intended audience of the text. Our analysis highlighted characteristics such as whether they were photographs, reproductions of art, cartoons, diagrams, or maps; whether they were captioned or not; whether related or unrelated to information given in the text; and whether they added new information or repeated information from the text. We counted the number of each.

Overall, we found a high number of illustrations, around one per page, in the books for all grades — 4, 8, and 11 — with little difference between grades. Where differences were found, they were between books intended for above-average and below-average readers in the same grade. The "lower" social studies textbooks had more photographs than the "higher," and the "higher" textbooks had more maps and diagrams. The "higher" science books within a grade had more relevant illustrations and used these illustrations as further explanations of the text. The "lower" science textbooks more often used illustrations to interest students and to introduce new information. Overall, there seemed to be a tendency for the illustrations in the books for lower achievers in each grade to be more concrete. In those meant for higher achievers, the illustrations tended to be more abstract, containing more maps and diagrams.

These findings were similar to those for questions: The books meant for the lower achievers tended to ask more factual, concrete questions as opposed to questions that require higher levels of cognitive processing. The question analysis was undertaken to assess the level of comprehension (i.e., the kind of cognitive reaction to the text) required by the questions in the books and workbooks. We were interested in any associations between the

demands of questions and differences in the books in terms of grade placement, content, publishers' designated audience, and readability scores.
The results of these analyses are reported later in this chapter.

The Dale-Chall readability formula was also applied to the 1985–1989
collection of books.* We then analyzed ten more comparable books, in
pairs representing the two time periods in question. This analysis was done
more qualitatively, to find any subtle changes that might not have been
picked up in the readability analysis.

SAMPLE ONE: BOOKS PUBLISHED BETWEEN 1974 AND 1982

In this section we report the results of our analysis of the difficulty of
fourth-, eighth- and eleventh-grade science and social studies books published between 1974 and 1982. We then compare these books to an estimate of the reading achievement levels of students in the corresponding
three grades and discuss the extent of challenge the books might offer for
average, above-average, and below-average readers. As an indicator of
students' reading abilities, we use the norms from the reading subtest of the
Metropolitan Achievement Test (1978), one of the most widely used standardized tests.

Fourth-Grade Textbooks

The fourth-grade sample consisted of 18 books: 10 social studies books
and 8 science books. Four of the books were classified by the publishers as
intended for a wide audience, nine were for below-average readers, and
five were for above-average readers.

Grade-equivalent scores from the readability analysis (see Table 5.1)
show that 9 of the 10 social studies books were one grade band above the
target grade level; only one, a book for below-average readers, scored at a
fourth-grade level. Scores for science books were evenly divided between
one grade band (5–6) and two grade bands (7–8) higher than the intended
grade level of their readers.

These fourth-grade books thus ranged in difficulty from a fourth- to an
eighth-grade level. The science books were consistently harder than the

---

*It should be noted that the new Dale-Chall formula, in press at this writing, was
available for experimental use when the textbooks published during 1985 to 1989 were analyzed. We decided, however, to use the original formula (Dale & Chall, 1948) in order to keep
the scores comparable with those from the earlier textbooks we analyzed—those published
between 1974 and 1982—and those reported in our previous study for 1945 to 1975 (Chall et
al., 1977).

TABLE 5.1: Dale-Chall Readability Scores for Fourth-Grade Books Published Between 1974 and 1982 ($N = 18$)

SUBJECT/ Intended Audience	Book Number	Grade-Equivalent (Readability) Scores*
SOCIAL STUDIES ($n = 10$)		
Wide audience	4-A	5-6
	4-B	5-6
Below-average readers	4-C	4th and Below
	4-D	5-6
	4-E	5-6
	4-F	5-6
	4-G	5-6
	4-H	5-6
Above-average readers	4-I	5-6
	4-J	5-6
SCIENCE ($n = 8$)		
Wide audience	4-K	5-6
	4-L	7-8
Below-average readers	4-M	5-6
	4-N	7-8
	4-O	7-8
Above-average readers	4-P	5-6
	4-Q	5-6
	4-R	7-8

*Grade-equivalent (readability) scores for each book represent the mean score of 8 to 10 sample passages in that book.

social studies, but in neither subject did difficulty vary according to particular audiences. In fact, science books specified for below-average readers were as difficult, and oftentimes more difficult, than those intended for above-average readers.

A reading-stage analysis (see Appendix D–2) was conducted on two science and two social studies books at each grade level, to confirm or disconfirm readability findings. To gain the broadest representation, the books analyzed were those intended for above- and below-average readers. Table 5.2 shows that findings for fourth-grade books were consistent with the readability findings. This more comprehensive and qualitative evaluation of the demands of fourth-grade textbooks also indicates that these books are probably above grade level in difficulty.

We also counted the number of illustrations in these four books. As shown in Table 5.2, three of the four books contained more than one illustration per page, and the average for the fourth was only slightly lower. Social studies books had relatively more illustrations than science

TABLE 5.2: Reading Stage and Illustration Analysis of Fourth-Grade Books Published Between 1974 and 1982

Subject/ Intended Audience	Stage Number and Grade*	Readability Score	Illustrations per Page
SOCIAL STUDIES (*n* = 2)			
Above-average readers	3A (4-6)	5-6	1.7
Below-average readers	3A (4-6)	5-6	1.1
SCIENCE (*n* = 2)			
Above-average readers	3A (4-6)	5-6	1.2
Below-average readers	3A (4-6)	7-8	.9

*Corresponding reading grade level of stage.

books, and books for above-average readers had more than those for below-average readers. Illustrations in all the books were quite similar; generally, they were photographs that reinforced information presented in the text, rather than adding new information.

Our analysis of the types of questions found in three of these fourth-grade social studies books showed that they did not differ on the whole according to the level of the readers to whom they were targeted (see Table 5.3). Over two-thirds of the questions in these three social studies books were noninferential, calling primarily for the recall of facts. Questions in the fourth-grade science book intended for a wide audience were also mainly for recall of facts, but those targeted to above- and below-average readers differed noticeably. Almost all the questions in the book for less able readers were factual, while the majority of those in the book for better readers called for inferences.

In summary, the stage analysis was consistent with the readability findings for the fourth-grade books. The findings for questions and illustrations were less clear cut. However, there seemed to be a tendency for the books meant for the lower achievers at this grade to have more concrete questions and illustrations than those meant for the higher achievers.

Eighth-Grade Textbooks

The eighth-grade sample included eight social studies books, two published for a wide audience, three for below-average readers, and three for above-average readers. The seven science books included two for a wide audience, two for below-average readers, and three for above-average readers.

Results of the readability analysis (see Table 5.4) indicated that scores for five of the eight social studies textbooks were on grade level, earning a

TABLE 5.3: Question Analysis of Fourth-Grade Books Published Between 1974 and 1982 (*N* = 6)

SUBJECT/ Intended Audience	Readability Score of Book	Number of Questions Analyzed*	Level of Questions	
			1 Fact	2, 3, 4 Inference
SOCIAL STUDIES (*n* = 3)				
Wide audience	5-6	57	70	30
Above-average readers	5-6	36	69	31
Below-average readers	5-6	22	68	32
SCIENCE (*n* = 3)				
Wide audience	7-8	23	74	26
Above-average readers	5-6	16	44	56
Below-average readers	7-8	31	94	6

*For this analysis, we used the questions in the middle chapter of each book.

7–8 grade-equivalent score. Two books were below grade level (5–6), and one was above (9–10). These books, then, offered a range of difficulty from fifth to tenth grade, although those intended for above- and below-average readers had about the same readability scores.

Five of the seven science books scored one grade band above grade level (9–10), and one book scored two grade bands higher (11–12). One book was on grade level (7–8). The books scoring the lowest and highest (7–8; 11–12) were the two designated for below-average readers. Overall, the sample of eighth-grade science books offered a range from seventh to twelfth grade, although, as with fourth-grade books, higher or lower readability scores were not associated in any logical way with texts targeted to the better or poorer readers. Among the eighth-grade books, science books generally had higher grade-equivalent scores than social studies books.

Our reading-stage analysis of two eighth-grade social studies books produced findings that were consistent with readability levels (see Table 5.5). For the two science books we checked, however, the stages assigned were lower, suggesting that the overall conceptual demands of science books may be less than the formula scores indicated.

Like the fourth-grade books, the eighth-grade social studies and science books averaged at least one illustration per page (see Table 5.5). Photographs were the most common type of illustration in the two eighth-grade social studies books we examined; in the two science books, there were also many charts and diagrams.

Table 5.6 shows the proportions of the two types of questions we analyzed in the books for both subjects. The majority of those in the books for wide audiences and for below-average readers were factual, especially in the science books. In both the social studies and science books for above-average readers, there was a shift toward more questions asking for infer-

TABLE 5.4: **Dale-Chall Readability Scores for Eighth-Grade Books Published Between 1974 and 1982 (*N* = 15)**

SUBJECT/ Intended Audience	Book Number	Grade-Equivalent (Readability) Scores*
SOCIAL STUDIES (*n* = 8)		
Wide audience	8-A	7-8
	8-B	9-10
Below-average readers	8-C	5-6
	8-D	7-8
	8-E	7-8
Above-average readers	8-F	5-6
	8-G	7-8
	8-H	7-8
SCIENCE (*n* = 7)		
Wide audience	8-I	9-10
	8-J	9-10
Below-average readers		
	8-K	7-8
	8-L	11-12
Above-average readers	8-M	9-10
	8-N	9-10
	8-O	9-10

*Grade-equivalent (readability) scores for each book represent the mean score of 8 to 10 sample passages in that book.

ences. This difference was especially noticeable in the social studies book.

Findings from the illustrations do not reveal clear trends, only that science books generally have more illustrations than the social studies books. There is also a tendency for the books meant for above-average readers to have more illustrations than those designed for the below-average readers. As for questions, the science books contained more factual

TABLE 5.5: **Reading Stage and Illustration Analysis of Eighth-Grade Books Published Between 1974 and 1982 (*N* = 4)**

SUBJECT/ Intended Audience	Stage Number and Grade*	Readability Score	Illustrations per Page
SOCIAL STUDIES (*n* = 2)			
Above-average readers	3B (7-8)	7-8	1.4
Below-average readers	3A (4-6)	5-6	1.0
SCIENCE (*n* = 2)			
Above-average readers	3B (7-8)	9-10	2.0
Below-average readers	3A (4-6)	7-8	1.6

*Corresponding reading grade level of stage.

TABLE 5.6: Question Analysis of Eighth-Grade Books Published Between 1974 and 1982 (*N* = 6)

Subject/ Intended Audience	Readability Score of Book	Number of Questions Analyzed*	Level of Questions 1 Fact	Level of Questions 2, 3, 4 Inference
Social Studies (*n* = 3)				
Wide audience	9-10	64	70	30
Above-average readers	7-8	38	26	74
Below-average readers	5-6	15	67	33
Science (*n* = 3)				
Wide audience	9-10	47	94	6
Above-average readers	9-10	25	60	40
Below-average readers	7-8	24	88	12

*For this analysis, we used the questions in the middle chapter of each book.

questions than social studies books. For both science and social studies books, those meant for above-average readers had more inferential questions than those for below-average readers.

Eleventh-Grade Textbooks

In the sample of 13 eleventh-grade books, 3 were for a wide audience, 6 for below-average readers, and 4 for above-average. Readability findings for the total sample are shown in Table 5.7.

Among the social studies books, the readability scores of two were on grade level (11–12). All the rest were below grade level; four were one grade band lower (9–10), and one was two grade bands lower (7–8). Among the science books, the tendency was just the opposite: Four of the six were above grade level, one scoring at a college graduate level (16 +). Eleventh-grade social studies books, therefore, offered a range from seventh to twelfth grades, although almost three-quarters of them were below grade level. Science books ranged from ninth grade to college graduate level.

Unlike science books for the earlier grades, the most difficult of the eleventh-grade books were intended for above-average readers. This was also true of social studies books, but to a lesser degree.

Our reading-stage analysis of two of the eleventh-grade social studies books produced results that were consistent with their readability levels (see Table 5.8). In the two science books we examined, however, reading-stage estimates were lower than readability scores, as was found in the eighth-grade sample.

Table 5.8 also shows that eleventh-grade books had fewer illustrations than fourth- and eighth-grade books. The social studies books contained a

TABLE 5.7: Dale-Chall Readability Scores for Eleventh-Grade Books Published Between 1974 and 1982 (N = 13)

Subject/ Intended Audience	Book Number	Grade-Equivalent (Readability) Scores*
Social Studies (n = 7)		
Wide audience	11-A	9-10
	11-B	11-12
Below-average readers	11-C	7-8
	11-D	9-10
	11-E	9-10
Above-average readers	11-F	9-10
	11-G	11-12
Science (n = 6)		
Wide audience	11-H	13-15
Below-average readers	11-I	9-10
	11-J	11-12
	11-K	13-15
Above-average readers	11-L	13-15
	11-M	16+

*Grade-equivalent (readability) scores for each book represent the mean score of 8 to 10 smaple passages in that book.

variety of illustrations, maps, cartoons, classic art, and photographs. Once again, like books for lower grades, science books contained photographs and charts or diagrams almost exclusively. In books for better readers in both subjects, illustrations were usually elaborations of text-presented information. In books for less able readers, however, illustrations were about evenly divided between those reinforcing information given in the text and those presenting new information.

Findings from the analysis of questions in the six eleventh-grade books, shown in Table 5.9, indicate that social studies books for below-average readers contained much larger percentages of factual questions than those for above-average readers or those for a wide audience. Factual questions outnumbered inferential questions in the science book for below-average readers as well, but this was also the case in the book for above-average readers. This finding also occurred in the eighth-grade social studies sample and suggests that books similar in readability may be more or less difficult depending on the kinds of questions they include.

From our readability analysis, then, we found eleventh-grade social studies books to be generally below grade level and science books to be generally above. Stage-analysis scores, however, suggested the science books may be less difficult when viewed more conceptually and holistically. The social studies book for below-average readers had more illustrations and more factual questions than the other two we examined. The science

TABLE 5.8: Reading Stage and Illustration Analysis of Eleventh-Grade Books Published Between 1974 and 1982 ($N = 4$)

SUBJECT/ Intended Audience	Stage Number and Grade*	Readability Score	Illustrations per Page
SOCIAL STUDIES ($n = 2$)			
Above-average readers	4 (9-12)	11-12	.6
Below-average readers	4 (9-12)	9-10	1.1
SCIENCE ($n = 2$)			
Above-average readers	4 (9-12)	16+	1.4
Below-average readers	3B (7-8)	9-10	.9

*Corresponding reading grade level of stage.

books were more like all the books for the lower grades in terms of illustrations; that is, slightly more were in the book for above-average readers.

Summary of Text Analyses

In considering the characteristics of all the books analyzed, we found science books to be more difficult than social studies books across the three grades. The difficulty of the books by readability scores was generally substantiated by our stage analysis, except for eighth- and eleventh-grade science books. This interesting difference may come from the nature of scientific writing. That is, technical terms in science are generally defined, discussed, and repeated often in a text. Such features lead to higher quantitative readability scores but to lower levels on the qualitative reading-stage

TABLE 5.9: Question Analysis of Eleventh-Grade Books Published Between 1974 and 1982 ($N = 6$)

SUBJECT/ Intended Audience	Readability Score of Book	Number of Questions Analyzed	Level of Questions 1 Fact	2, 3, 4 Inference
SOCIAL STUDIES ($n = 3$)				
Wide audience	11-12	128	54	46
Above-average readers	11-12	23	39	61
Below-average readers	9-10	14	93	7
SCIENCE ($n = 3$)				
Wide audience	13-15	2	____*	____*
Above-average readers	16+	87	70	30
Below-average readers	9-10	17	76	24

*Findings for this book are not reported since they were of questionable validity. For this analysis, we used the questions in the middle chapter of each book; this book had only two questions there.

analysis. In contrast, the text of social studies books may be more difficult than the quantitative formulas indicate, since much of the vocabulary has generic meaning as well as specific meaning within the subject. For example, *cabinet, appeal,* and *movement* are not difficult terms in a general sense, but are more difficult when used as specific technical terms in social studies. Such terms are not "picked up" as different, nor are they defined or repeated in the text, which would make them more comprehensible.

In general, all the books we analyzed were widely illustrated; they usually contained at least one illustration per page of text. Contrary to what might have been expected, however, books intended for the better readers tended to have the most illustrations.

Fourth-grade books were more difficult for fourth-grade students than were the books for the students in the two higher grades. They offered the narrowest range — three grade levels. Both the eighth- and eleventh-grade books had wider ranges: 5–6 to 11–12 for eighth grade and 7–8 to 16 + for eleventh grade.

The kinds of questions asked in the texts varied by their intended readers. Books for less able readers included more factual and fewer inferential questions than those for better readers or wide audiences. As we discussed earlier, since factual questions are generally known to be easier than inferential questions, this may be a way to make the books less demanding, although the effects of such a practice may lead to less than desirable outcomes.

Level of Challenge: A Comparison with Test Norms

What was the level of challenge of these books for students of different reading abilities? To answer this question, we compared the books' readability scores to the norms of the Metropolitan Achievement Test (MAT). Grade-equivalent scores were used for both. To represent average achievement, we used the 50th-percentile MAT score, the mean of the scores for that grade. To represent below-average achievement, we used the 24th-percentile score, and for above-average achievement, the 76th-percentile score. Table 5.10 shows the actual scores for these three levels of readers, at the three grade levels we studied. For example, at the beginning of Grade 4, the grade-equivalent score for average fourth-grade students was 3.8, while the below-average scored at high second grade (2.6) and the above-average scored at low sixth grade (6.1). Scores for the other two grades may be read similarly.

Our discussion of these scores compared to the difficulty of the textbooks analyzed will be done by grade, since we have already reported that

TABLE 5.10: Mean Reading Scores in Grade Equivalents for Low, Average, and High Percentiles on the Metropolitan Achievement Test

| | | Grade Equivalent Scores | | |
| | | Below Avg. | Average | Above Avg. |
Grade	*(MAT* Percentile:)*	*(24th)*	*(50th)*	*(76th)*
Fourth grade (Elementary)		2.6	3.8	6.1
Eighth grade (Advanced 1)		5.7	8.3	11.2
Eleventh grade (Advanced 2)		8.5	11.3	12+

*Forms JS and KS, 1978 edition; norms for fall administration.

the difficulty of the books varied in relation to the grade for which they were intended (the lower the grade, the greater the relative difficulty of the books). Readers should refer back to Tables 5.1, 5.4, and 5.7.

Fourth-grade books were above the reading abilities of most of the students who took the MAT. Overall, the readability scores of these books were at the fifth- to sixth-grade level, with a range from the fourth grade to the eighth grade. Comparing these scores to those in Table 5.10, it can be seen that the textbooks would probably be difficult for the average students and extremely difficult for the below-average. Only the above-average, who scored 6.1, would be fairly well matched.

The eighth-grade books offered a more realistic level of challenge to most eighth graders, as their readability scores ranged mostly from the seventh- through tenth-grade levels, with extremes from fifth to twelfth grade. The average readability score of the books for the eighth grade was thus also above the average MAT grade-equivalent score of 8.3, but the gap was considerably smaller than for fourth graders. Below-average students in this grade would find the books very difficult, while the above-average quarter would find the books well within their reading ability.

Taking a look next at the match for eleventh-grade students, we found that about half of their books were at a tenth-grade or lower level in readability; the other half were at an eleventh-grade level or higher. Comparing these figures with those in Table 5.10, it can be seen that the average eleventh-grade student would be challenged by some of these books but not by others. Once again, readers scoring in the lowest quarter on the MAT would have difficulty with most of the books for their grade. Finally, about three-quarters of the books would be very easy for above-average students.

To summarize, fourth-grade books would probably be difficult for all but the upper quarter in reading achievement. Most of the eighth-grade books would be appropriate in difficulty for average students and somewhat easy for the upper quarter. Only a few would be appropriate for students in the lower quarter of reading achievement. For eleventh-grade students in the lower quarter of the achievement range, most books would be somewhat to very challenging. For average eleventh-grade students, the books would be easily within their reading levels, while for students in the upper quarter of achievement, most would offer little challenge.

Impressionistic Assessment

To gain a still broader perspective of the books, we offer an impressionistic assessment of the many features that are often addressed in discussions of textbook quality. Quality is a complex attribute that we hypothesize encompasses many dimensions, including physical characteristics, structure, content, and style, as well as readability. Indeed, writing of high quality can be found at all levels of difficulty and maturity, from the beginner books of Dr. Seuss and Else Minarik to the complex novels of William Faulkner. Low-quality writing that represents this span can also be found.

First, the size of the textbooks in this sample was striking. The fourth-grade social studies and science books we analyzed averaged about 300 pages. Eighth-grade books typically ran 700 pages, and 1,000 was the norm for eleventh-grade books. The sheer weight of these books, especially in the upper two grades, was remarkable in itself. If students carried them from school to home and back for homework assignments, the physical load was considerable.

All books were profusely illustrated and contained a variety of teaching and learning aids, including questions for reading comprehension, for vocabulary development, and for using study skills. Follow-up suggestions included a wide array of activities, but we could find few suggestions for writing or for setting priorities (i.e., for determining what in the massive textbooks and accompanying workbooks was most important and why).

For each grade, the books presented a myriad of topics, particularly in social studies. The introduction to one fourth-grade text described its content as including history, geography, civics and government, economics, and sociology. The book was organized into 10 chapters, ranging from "Living on the Planet Earth" and "People Shape Their Environment" to "Living in Your Community and State" and "Learning to Live in Peace." Another fourth-grade social studies text contained nine units and 26 chapters covering the world's continents (e.g., the Middle East), major areas, and countries, including Saudi Arabia, Nigeria, Greece, and Czechoslovakia.

Is it possible for teachers to teach — and for fourth-grade students to learn — so much varied content in one year? Because of the textbooks' broad coverage and varied content, most topics received only perfunctory treatment, emerging as little more than lists of facts loosely related to a theme. The following excerpt from a fourth-grade social studies textbook shows the rather sparse treatment of ideas. The italics are ours and indicate different concepts, each worthy of more explanation.

> It seems to us that *the earth stands quite still.* But it is *really moving all the time.* You know it is *moving around the sun.* The earth moves *another way too.*
>
> The earth rotates, or turns *around an imaginary line through its center.* We call this line its *axis* (ak′ sus). The *North Pole* is at one end of the *axis.* The *South Pole* is on the other end.

Is it necessary to introduce ideas in history and geography with ideas from astronomy that are also new and need explanation? This excerpt recalls an observation about social studies textbooks made some 60 years ago by Ernest Horn (1937). They are difficult, he said, because they cover a century and a half in a page and a half, without really explaining and teaching. Horn was describing a shortcoming that has come to be known as "mentioning" — the coverage of many topics, but only in a very perfunctory way (Tyson-Bernstein, 1988).

The eighth-grade social studies textbooks were even more comprehensive than the fourth-grade ones. One contained 30 chapters, starting with "Land and First Americans" and concluding with "Challenge of the 80's." Like many other eighth-grade texts, it seemed to assume that it was "teaching from scratch," that students would bring no previous knowledge to the organized knowledge of the text. Yet the writing style was not didactic, tending toward the breezy, bantering tone found in popular magazines.

Why social studies textbooks cover so many different ideas in space and time, in geographic regions, and in social theories is one of the many complex questions about textbooks. Is it to satisfy the social studies curriculum requirements in all of the 50 states? In Chapter 9, we examine what aspects of these books textbook-adoption committees evaluate and the criteria they use. Each has strong requirements that differ by state or district; as we note, in order to be on the "approved list," publishers tend to include them all, often by simply making mention of them.

Perhaps this overabundance of topics can also be traced to the lack of consensus among social studies teachers, specialists, and administrators as to what the social studies curriculum should include at each grade level and from what viewpoint (e.g., from the perspective of a chronological "story" or from the standpoint of social issues).

Science textbooks seem not to suffer as much from this problem. They offer a more limited body of connected knowledge in a more logical, analytical manner. Science books also tend to be shorter in length. It seems that their mission is less broad than the social studies books, concentrating on one scientific discipline, such as earth science, physics, or chemistry.

SAMPLE TWO: BOOKS PUBLISHED BETWEEN 1985 AND 1989

In this section we present an analysis of 21 books published from 1985 to 1989; in the next section we compare them to the findings for the earlier sample. (See Appendix B–1 for a complete listing of the samples.) This second sample of books was published during and subsequent to a period of much professional and public debate about textbooks. One of the focal points of the attacks in newspapers, magazines, and commission reports was that the textbooks lacked rigor — that they were not sufficiently demanding. Harder books were recommended. Since these recommendations started in the late 1970s, it would seem that, by 1985 to 1989, publishers would have had sufficient time to make changes. Our question, then, was, Did publishers follow the recommendations for more demanding books?

As noted in the introduction to this chapter, the instrument used to analyze this second sample was the Dale-Chall readability formula. We examined three social studies and four science books for each grade; Table 5.11 shows their readability scores. The mean score for fourth-grade social studies textbooks was 5–6, and for science, 7–8. Thus, almost all of the fourth-grade books were above grade level; only one, a social studies book,

TABLE 5.11: Dale-Chall Readability Scores for Books Published Between 1985 and 1989 ($N = 21$)

Grade	Grade Equivalent (Readability) Scores	
	Social Studies	Science
Fourth grade ($n = 7$)	5-6	7-8
	4th and below	5-6
	5-6	7-8
		7-8
Eighth grade ($n = 7$)	7-8	9-10
	7-8	9-10
	7-8	9-10
		9-10
Eleventh grade ($n = 7$)	11-12	13-15
	7-8	11-12
	9-10	13-15
		11-12

scored at the target grade level. Science books were more difficult than social studies books.

The mean score for eighth-grade social studies books was 7–8, and for science, 9–10. Social studies books were therefore on grade level, while science books were one grade band higher.

The mean score for eleventh-grade social studies books was 9–10, while that for science books fell between 11–12 and 13–15. Social studies books were therefore below grade level, and science books, on or somewhat above grade level.

A COMPARISON OF BOOKS OVER A DECADE

In assessing how the textbooks published in the latter part of the 1980s compared with those published 10 to 15 years earlier, we compared the mean readability scores from earlier and later samples. We chose to use only sample 1 books that were intended for a wide audience. This was because sample 2 was recommended by publishers as those used by the widest audience; none of them was intended for above- or below-average readers.

Grade-equivalent scores for the two samples are presented in Table 5.12. As can be seen, the fourth- and eighth-grade books for both were identical; thus the difficulty of the books had not changed over the years, according to the readability analysis. The rigor — the demands on students — remained essentially the same.

The eleventh-grade textbooks did seem to show a change in readability, but in a direction counter to the recommendations for greater rigor and challenge. Indeed, the eleventh-grade textbooks published between 1985

TABLE 5.12: Mean Dale-Chall Readability Scores of Wide-Audience Books Published Between 1974 and 1982 and Between 1985 and 1989

| GRADE/Subject | Mean Dale-Chall Readability Scores (Grade-Equivalent) | | | |
| | 1974-1982 | | 1985-1989 | |
	n	Scores	n	Scores
FOURTH GRADE				
Social Studies	2	5-6	3	5-6
Science	2	7-8	4	7-8
EIGHTH GRADE				
Social Studies	1	7-8	3	7-8
Science	2	9-10	4	9-10
ELEVENTH GRADE				
Social Studies	1	11-12	3	9-10
Science	2	13-15	4	11-12

and 1989 were even less challenging for average eleventh graders than those published earlier, according to the readability analysis.

Overall, the readability levels of the more recently published books were similar to those for the earlier books. As was the case for those published in the early 1980s, science books were more difficult than the social studies books. Fourth-grade books were more difficult relative to the reading abilities of students who used them than were books for the eighth and eleventh grades. Science and social studies textbooks were generally on or above grade level in Grades 4 and 8. Only eleventh-grade social studies books were, on the average, below grade level.

A COMPARISON OF PAIRS OF BOOKS BY THE SAME PUBLISHER

We present here a comparison of five pairs of books. Each pair contains one book from the earlier sample and one from the later. Both are written for the same grade, on the same subject, and by the same publisher. In only one comparison (Publisher E: eleventh-grade science text) was the newer book a revised edition of the older one. Nevertheless, a comparison of the mean readability scores of each pair of books (see Table 5.13) indicated great similarity in difficulty, consistent with the findings just reported in Table 5.12.

In addition to this quantitative analysis, we made some qualitative comparisons designed to pick up any evidence of other, more subtle changes in the difficulty of the earlier and later editions of these books. We present our results here according to the publisher of each pair of books.

Publisher A

The first pair of books compared were fourth-grade science books; one was published in 1980, the other in 1985. The two were written by essentially the same team of authors, although copyright information shows the later book to be new rather than a revision of the earlier one. The books had different titles (only the 1985 book bears the publisher's name), but covered almost the same content in eight similarly named units. The 1985 book was slightly longer, up from 310 to 346 pages.

Illustrations in the new book had been updated, and there seemed to be more of them, particularly on the introductory pages. Questions that appeared at the end of the units had also been updated, but a small-scale comparison indicated the ratio of factual to inferential questions was essentially unchanged. A significant change had been made, however, in the headings for the questions. In the earlier book, the title given the questions

TABLE 5.13: Mean Dale-Chall Readability Scores of Books Published Between 1974 and 1982 and Between 1985 and 1989, from the Same Publisher, for the Same Grade and Subject

PUBLISHER/ Grade and Subject	Copyright Date	Grade-Equivalent (Readability) Score
PUBLISHER A		
Fourth-grade science[a]		
Book 1	1980	5-6
Book 2	1985	5-6
PUBLISHER B		
Fourth-grade science[a]		
Book 1	1980	7-8
Book 2	1989	7-8
PUBLISHER C		
Eighth-grade social studies[a]		
Book 1	1982	7-8
Book 2	1986	7-8
PUBLISHER D		
Eleventh-grade social studies[a]		
Book 1	1982	9-10
Book 2	1986	9-10
PUBLISHER E		
Eleventh-grade science[b]		
Book 1	1979	13-15
Book 2	1987	13-15

[a]New edition.   [b]Revised edition.

was "Looking Back." In the later edition it was, "Check-Up Time: Vocabulary, Facts, Concepts," with the same questions sorted to represent the three categories. This difference in labels for essentially the same questions suggests that publishers are very aware of the recent emphasis on reading comprehension and higher-level thinking processes and that teachers prefer a variety of questions of increasing complexity.

We also noted some changes in the writing of the later edition that suggested attention to the concept of "considerateness" of text in terms of cohesion and coherence, as described by Armbruster (1984). In a discussion of the nature of salmon, for example, the earlier text began with little introduction: "Now the salmon spawn. That is, the female salmon lays eggs. The male salmon lays sperm over the eggs." The newer book read: "At last the salmon that are left reach the places where they were hatched. Here the salmon spawn. That is, the female salmon lays eggs. Then the male salmon lays sperm over the eggs."

Later, in the older book, the salmon's nest is described as follows: "The salmon make a kind of nest for the eggs. Both salmon swim along one place on the bottom, moving their heads and tails from side to side. In this way, they clear out a long hollow in the river bed." The newer book added more detail, seemingly for the purpose of making new concepts more understandable: "Before laying their eggs, the salmon make a kind of nest. Both salmon swim along one spot at the bottom, moving their heads and tails from side to side. In this way they clear out a long hollow on the river bottom." These changes, it seems, fit quite nicely within the category of more "considerate" text, a term currently favored by many psychologists, as well as more "user-friendly," a label preferred by computer specialists.

Publisher B

Our second comparison was also of fourth-grade science books, the first published in 1980 and the second in 1989. The titles of the books differed; the name of the publisher was not part of the older title. The senior author of the earlier book had died in the interim; the two others were the same for both books. The newer book was longer than the older by 76 pages (up from 300 to 376 pages), although it covered approximately the same content in nine similarly named units. The 1989 book included more special features, such as "Science and Technology" and "Language Arts Skills." Another addition was a statement of learning goals.

The newer book asked more questions, set in the margins of the text and in the chapter and unit reviews. Instead of simply listing vocabulary words to be learned, as in the earlier book, the new one gave fill-in-the-blank exercises for practice. Both books had many illustrations, but the newer had a more sophisticated look, due to the appearance of its print and margins. It also seemed to provide more details about each topic covered. For example, the earlier book's discussion of the eye read: "Light enters your eyes through the pupil. The pupil is the black, round opening in the center of the colored part of the eye. It is like a window." In the newer book the discussion seemed to be more specific and elaborate, and to spread difficult concepts over more sentences: "Light enters your eyes through the pupils. The pupil is the clear opening in the center of the iris of the eye. It looks black. The amount of light that enters the eye changes when the size of the pupil is changed by the movement of the iris."

This pair of books also provided an example of how newer books seem to be "up-to-the-minute" in terms of current social interest. The human body and good health were the topics of the final unit in both books, but the concepts emphasized and the extent of coverage were quite different. In the 1980 book, the unit began with a discussion of body structure (cells, tissues, organs) and systems (circulatory, skeletal, digestive). It later covered body care, but that part contained only nine pages of text and discussed exercise, sleep, cleanliness, and proper diet, mainly in terms of food groups. In the newer book, the unit's initial focus was on the importance of good health habits, in this case stressing exercise, weight control, sleep, and skin care. The next part, however, was completely devoted to healthy eating and was 32 pages in all. These differences seem to be consistent with today's concerns for healthful habits, particularly those related to food and weight control.

Publisher C

This third comparison was of eighth-grade social studies books, the first published in 1982 and the second in 1986. Although the publisher was the same, the books differed in name and authorship. The 1986 book was longer by more than 150 pages, up from 627 to 786 pages. It was more colorful, more sophisticated in appearance, and included many added special features. While chapters in the earlier book began with a story, chapters in the newer one began with descriptions of content, outlines, and time lines. The newer book asked more questions, both after individual sections within chapters and at the ends of units. While there were more questions, the proportion of factual to inferential questions was about the same as that in the earlier book. The newer book gave more explicit attention to skill improvement, both for learning history and for improving reading.

Similar content was covered in both books, but the newer one seemed to provide more detail, as the following examples from descriptions of the Lewis and Clark expedition show. The 1982 text read:

> "Look for the woman!" This is an old saying. It means that whenever you read or hear about a man who does something great, be on the lookout for the woman who helped him. This story is about a woman — an Indian woman — who helped a whole group of men, and the nation too. The men were the members of the Lewis and Clark expedition.
>
> In 1803 Meriwether Lewis and William Clark were sent by President Thomas Jefferson to explore the lands west of the Mississippi. Along with their expedition of 29 men, they explored the northwestern part of what is now the United States. They brought back much information about the Louisiana Territory, which Jefferson had just purchased from France. Through part of this long and dangerous journey their guide was a young Indian woman, Sacajawea.

The 1986 text seemed more straightforward. It gave more detail about the ages and occupations of the explorers and their tasks, and even specified Clark's kinship to a hero of the Revolutionary War:

Jefferson appointed as leaders of the expedition the 32-year-old Meriwether Lewis, who first learned wilderness skills in the Blue Ridge Mountains of Virginia, and a 28-year-old scout and soldier named William Clark. Clark's older brother, George Rogers Clark, was the hero who had captured Vincennes during the Revolution.

Congress instructed Lewis and Clark to make maps of the areas they visited. They were also to keep careful records of animal and vegetable life and of minerals and soils they saw on their journey. Congress also said the explorers should speak with Indian leaders they met about trade with the United States.

The Lewis and Clark expedition, consisting of 48 men, set out from St. Louis in the spring of 1804.

Some of the differences in these two accounts may stem from a change in the target audience of the two books.* The 1982 book was identified as a book for below-average readers. The 1986 book is a best-seller, and therefore we assume it is intended for a more broad-based audience. Indeed, although the readability scores of the two are the same, the newer book has many characteristics of a more demanding book: It is longer, the print is smaller, more ideas about topics are included, and it asks more questions.

Publisher D

The two eleventh-grade social studies books compared here were published in 1982 and 1986. The titles differed, but the authors — renowned textbook writers and historians — were the same.

The books were almost identical in physical features, structure, content, illustrations, titles and numbers of units, and the text itself. To illustrate the consistency in the treatment of topics, we present the following excerpt from a discussion of the Lewis and Clark expedition that appears on different pages in the two books but is otherwise identical in every detail:

The Lewis and Clark expedition. Nobody knew the boundaries of Louisiana, although a few white trappers and many Indian tribes had some idea of what lay within the territory. Jefferson decided to explore the vast region that the nation had bought. He assigned the task to a United States army expedition led by Meriwether Lewis and William Clark (see map, this page).

The expedition of about 45 men left the Mississippi at St. Louis on May 14, 1804, and traveled up the Missouri River to its headwaters. There they hired Indian guides and horses and journeyed over perilous mountain trails to

---

*All books from the 1974–1982 sample that had a counterpart in the second sample were included in this comparison by publishers. Target audiences — whether a wide audience or above- or below-average readers — were not taken into account.

the headwaters of the Clearwater River. Then they built canoes and made their way down the Clearwater and the Columbia Rivers to the Pacific Ocean.

Questions in the two versions were also almost identical in number, placement, and type. In the newer one, however, the questions were labeled as calling either for analyzing ideas, summarizing ideas, or comparing ideas. But, as in the fourth-grade science textbooks compared earlier, this new concern with labeling the questions to indicate attention to various levels of thinking and questioning considered important in the recent literature on the teaching of reading did not seem to be reflected in any difference in the questions themselves. They were essentially the same as those in the earlier edition.

Other features had also been given new titles in the revised edition. "Developing History Study Skills" in the 1986 book, for example, was an exact replication of the 1982 book's "Developing Social Studies Skills." Why the change from social studies to history? Perhaps it is because of the current debate among professionals within the field, which seems to be favoring history instead of social studies.

The major difference in the two books was an increase of 180 pages in length — up from 880 to 1,060 pages. Some of these additional pages were designed to update historical information, but many of them seemed to be for additional illustrations in the introductions of units and chapters and additional special features such as "American Profiles," "Decision Moments," and "This Changing Land."

Although not the focus of our analysis, it seems important to note certain inconsistencies in the historical facts presented in these social studies books. Differences are quite obvious in the information they give about the number of men in the expedition as well as the date of its departure. Variations in emphasis on particular characters in this historical drama are also interesting. In one of the books, Sacajawea is the central character in the Lewis and Clark saga, whereas in the others, her contributions are noted but in much less detail.

Publisher E

The eleventh-grade science books compared here were revised editions, one published in 1979 and the other in 1987. The title and the authors of the two books were the same. The newer version was 29 pages longer, an increase from 635 to 664 pages.

The 1987 edition was similar in content to the 1979 edition, but topics had been added and chapters reorganized. The illustrations in the revised edition were occasionally repeated, but the majority were different. End-of-chapter questions were sometimes the same, but new ones had been added and others changed, in keeping with differences in organization. Another difference at the chapter level was the addition of vocabulary lists, although no directions were given for how these lists were to be used.

Both editions stated goals for each chapter; however, the newer one displayed these more prominently and stated them more clearly. The 1979 version read, "You will gain an understanding of the nature of chemistry through a study of the relationship between science and human progress." The 1987 version read, "You will gain an understanding of the nature of chemistry. You will examine the relationship between science and human progress. You will define matter and energy."

Overall, the two volumes were close in content, but the 1987 version presented a new and more colorful face. The major difference appeared in organization of the book as a whole and the identification of key scientific concepts. For example, in the 1979 book, a discussion of oxidation read as follows:

> Some hydrocarbons have very large heats of combustion. Thus, they are used commercially as fuels. Natural gas (methane) and bottled gas (butane containing some propane and ethane) are used in the home for heating and cooking. Ethane (acetylene) is used in cutting and welding torches.
>
> The heats of combustion for a number of common organic fuels are given in Table 24–6. The values are in units of kilojoules per mole. To find out which of several fuels would be the most economical, the price must be considered. If we know the price of the fuel per kilogram, we can convert the data as follows.
> . . .

This topic is treated quite similarly in the 1986 book, but changes in some words will be noted:

> Some hydrocarbons have very large enthalpies of combustion. Thus, they are used commercially as fuels. Natural gas (methane) and bottled gas (butane containing some propane and ethane) are used in the home for heating and cooking. Acetylene is used in cutting and welding torches.
>
> The enthalpies of combustion for a number of common organic fuels are given in Table 30–1, page 608. The values are in units of kj/mol. To find out which of several fuels would be the most economical, the price must be considered. If we know the price of the fuel per kilogram, we can convert the data as follows. . . .

Summary of Comparisons

What generalizations can be made about these earlier and later versions of social studies and science books? Did they change? If so, did the changes reflect those suggested by textbook reformers and critics?

The recommendations of the National Commission on Excellence in Education (1983) in *A Nation at Risk*, that textbooks become more rigorous and demanding, seem not to have been followed. Predictions that publishers were developing more difficult books (e.g., Trombley, 1982) are not borne out by our findings. Readability levels did not change in any appreciable way between the 1979 and the 1989 versions. Indeed, our qualitative analysis indicates that, where there were changes, they were toward greater ease, not greater difficulty. The general content and structure at the chapter and unit levels also did not seem to change.

There were some noticeable differences, however, particularly in length and appearance. The more recent books were clearly longer — from 29 to 180 pages longer. Similar to difficulty level, this change was in a direction opposite to that recommended.

Certain physical properties also changed. The newer books had more illustrations and were even more colorful than the earlier ones. Again, this seems to be counter to the current views, which often call into question the value of extensive illustrations.

The newer books looked more sophisticated, with smaller print and less extensive margins. The appearance of greater maturity was enhanced further by a greater abundance and variety of special features, including mini-lessons, small vignettes, biographies, and excerpts from historically significant speeches or documents.

More questions appeared in the newer books. Generally, the kinds of questions seemed unchanged from those in the earlier editions, but the way they were labeled seemed to have changed. The tendency seemed to be to label them as teaching higher-order thought processes. More questions appeared at the ends of chapters and units and at the beginnings and ends of sections. In some books, questions were also inserted in the margins alongside the text.

Newer books seemed also to include more details about particular topics. They elaborated more and seemed to have more cohesive ties and more text per concept. This is one area that seems consistent with reformers' recommendations that texts have more explicit structure and greater depth and engage in less "mentioning."

However well-intended, all these changes have resulted in books of greater size. Also, although the types of questions have not changed, asking *more* questions may make the books more demanding. On the other hand, books that are more colorful and more conspicuously illustrated and that have a "magazine-like" quality seem aimed toward greater ease. The increased attention to detail, elaboration, structure, and relationships among sentences also shows concern for the "considerateness" of the text.

Further, the newer books seem to pay more attention to aids that make them more "user friendly." For example, explicit statements of learning goals, outlines of content, and summary statements alongside paragraphs seem to remove much of the responsibility for learning from the student and transfer it to the text. One wonders if we will soon be hearing criticism about the "deskilling" of students, as we are now hearing that overly helpful teacher's manuals are "deskilling" teachers (Shannon, 1989).

Thus while many have called for more rigorous textbooks, our analyses of books published over the past decade show little change in readability. An impressionistic review of a more limited number of texts, however, revealed that there may be some qualitative differences in organization and cohesion, as well as greater concern for the teaching of vocabulary and comprehension.

PUBLISHERS SPEAK TO THE ISSUE IN TEACHER'S MANUALS

The results just described suggest that difficulty remains as much an issue for publishers today as it was in the early 1980s (see Chapter 10). Further evidence for this lies in the way publishers talked about difficulty in the teacher's manuals for both the earlier and later books (see Table 5.12).

In the teacher's editions for all books published around 1980, the difficulty of the student's book was described in terms of readability. In addition, the readability of the book was almost always mentioned in terms of "controlling" difficulty or insuring "easier" text. A few examples illustrate this quite clearly: "In controlling the reading level, careful attention has been given to vocabulary, sentence construction, paragraph structure, chapter organization and format." "Vocabulary and sentence length have been controlled using the Dale-Chall readability formula as a guide. Readability of text has been adjusted to provide for easier reading." "The text is clearly written and easy to understand. The level of readability has been carefully controlled."

Only one teacher's manual in the earlier sample took the "middle ground" with regard to readability: "A text that is too hard frustrates students; a text that is too easy bores them. [Our book] is neither too easy nor too hard."

Now let us see how the teacher's manuals for the textbooks published after 1985 address the issue of difficulty. Readability was mentioned explicitly in 3 of the 21 manuals, all for science textbooks published by the same company. The following paragraph appeared in the manuals for its fourth-, eighth-, and eleventh-grade textbooks:

> The importance of readability has been an underlying concern of the authors and editors of [this book]. For this reason, reading level has been carefully controlled throughout each level. . . . Several readability formulas have been

used to determine the average reading level range for each text. A variety of passages from each unit were tested. The readability scores were computed from an analysis of data employing such readability instruments as Spache, Fry, and Dale-Chall.

Most of the manuals for the books published toward the end of the 1980s described difficulty in terms other than readability, as the following examples illustrate:

> [This book] achieves its goals through its clear organization and highly readable text. . . . The authors have written the text in a lively narrative style.

> [This book] is written in clear, uncluttered prose. Its easy-to-follow style will heighten students' interest in the material and further their understanding as well.

> The range of content also allows for great flexibility. There is ample material to challenge students capable of rapid progress. The program also provides experiences that ensure success with less motivated students.

In other newer manuals, discussions of difficulty focused on "teachability":

> Great care has been taken to create a distinctly teachable text, one that will serve the needs of both teachers and students.

Thus, although the terms have changed, concern for difficulty remains an important issue for publishers and for the teachers who use their books.

It would seem that the negative attention to readability formulas has altered the terminology publishers use to discuss difficulty, but not, essentially, the measurement of difficulty and the difficulty of the textbooks themselves.

CHAPTER 6

Educating Teachers About Textbook Difficulty and Effective Textbook Use

This chapter is concerned with how teachers are informed about textbook difficulty and the matching of texts to student ability. Our method was to analyze the teacher's manuals accompanying the social studies and science textbooks we examined in Chapter 5, as well as the professional textbooks on methods of teaching social studies, science, and reading, for their information and suggestions to teachers on issues of text difficulty. (See Appendix B–2 for a bibliographic listing of the methods textbooks analyzed.)

We thought the teacher's manuals were important sources of information on what teachers learned about text difficulty, since they are designed by publishers to help teachers make the best use of their textbooks. We also considered professional methods textbooks another important source of information, since they are designed to convey to teachers the best practices for teaching, based on the best available research evidence.

In addition, the teacher's manuals were examined for their suggestions on the use of the textbooks for teaching vocabulary, comprehension strategies, study skills, and the like. We looked at these suggestions for teaching since, in a broad sense, the way teachers assist students in their reading of texts and other instructional materials affects the ease or difficulty of the texts for the students. With effective assistance from the teacher, a difficult text may become optimal for learning.

We also thought it important to know whether teachers received sufficient knowledge about textbooks, particularly about appropriate difficulty, since many people have been calling for more teacher participation on state textbook-adoption committees. They have also been recommending that teachers have the authority to select the textbooks for use in their own classes. Since teachers are, together with their students, the ultimate users of textbooks, by exercising discrimination they can be a force for the improvement of textbooks.

We present, first, our findings on the various issues of textbook difficulty covered in the teacher's manuals and methods textbooks. Then we present our findings on suggestions for effective textbook use, as given in the teacher's manuals. We conclude with a summary comparing the two types of books.

INFORMATION ON TEXT DIFFICULTY

Teacher's Manuals

Well over half of the 34 teacher's manuals accompanying the social studies and science textbooks (see Chapter 5) addressed the issue of text difficulty and the importance of a suitable match between students' reading abilities and text difficulty (see Table 6.1). These manuals drew teachers' attention to the issues by such statements as the following:

> Careful attention has been given to vocabulary, sentence construction, paragraph structure, sequencing, illustrations, and format. The vocabulary in the text is consistent with the developmental level of the students for whom it is designed.

> Language and style are simple. . . . Many names, terms, and other details

TABLE 6.1: **Percentage of Teacher's Manuals for Fourth-, Eighth-, and Eleventh-Grade Social Studies and Science Textbooks Giving Attention to Text Difficulty and Various Matching Procedures**

	Social Studies				Science				All Manuals
	Gr. 4 (n=9)	Gr. 8 (n=7)	Gr. 11 (n=2)	Tot. (n=18)	Gr. 4 (n=5)	Gr. 8 (n=7)	Gr. 11 (n=4)	Tot. (n=16)	(N=34)
Attention given to difficulty	67	29	50	62	80	84	50	75	62
PROCEDURES SUGGESTED									
Readability formulas	56	14	50	39	100	43	25	56	47
Standardized tests	11	14	0	11	20	0	0	6	9
Cloze procedure	0	0	0	0	20	14	0	12	6
"Try-outs" with students	0	14	0	6	20	14	25	18	12
Informal reading inventories	11	14	0	11	20	0	0	6	9
Adjust match during lesson	11	43	0	22	40	29	0	24	24

traditionally found in American history texts have been omitted because they increase difficulty but are not essential to understanding.

Some of the manuals wrote of using formulas to control vocabulary and sentence length, a purpose for which these formulas were never intended: "To help insure ease of readability, vocabulary and sentence length have been controlled according to formulas." Another noted, "Extra space has been inserted between words to ensure ease of reading."

Overall, elementary-level manuals were more likely to discuss a concern for matching textbook difficulty to students' reading levels than were secondary-level manuals. Almost half of all the manuals recommended readability formulas to assess difficulty of texts and as a way of matching students and texts. Other procedures mentioned for effecting a suitable match included the use of standardized or teacher-made tests (usually of a fill-in-the-blank type), tryouts of portions of the text with students, and the administration of individual reading inventories, an informal type of assessment.

About one-quarter of the manuals suggested ways to adjust textbooks to students of varying abilities. These included ability grouping, the use of supplementary materials, easier books for poorer readers, and rewriting or simplifying difficult texts. But no criteria were suggested for optimal matching; that is, nothing was said about the levels of text difficulty that would be most suitable for given levels of reading ability.

Social Studies and Science Methods Textbooks

The methods textbooks in social studies and science generally gave similar suggestions to teachers regarding the assessment of text difficulty (see Table 6.2), although these appeared less frequently than in the teacher's manuals. For example, one-half of the teacher's manuals mentioned using techniques such as readability formulas for estimating text difficulty, but only about one-quarter of the social studies methods books and none of

TABLE 6.2: Percentage of Social Studies, Science, and Reading Methods Textbooks Including Information About Assessing Difficulty, Matching, and Optimal Difficulty ($N = 51$)

| | Content Area Textbooks | | | | | | Reading ($n = 29$) | |
| | Social Studies ($n = 14$) | | Science ($n = 8$) | | Total ($n = 22$) | | | |
Topic	n	%	n	%	n	%	n	%
Assessing difficulty	4	29	0	0	4	18	18	62
Matching methods	13	93	6	75	19	86	23	79
Optimal difficulty	0	0	0	0	0	0	15	52

the science methods textbooks mentioned using such assessment procedures. With regard to matching texts to students of varying needs, however, more of the content methods textbooks than teacher's manuals offered suggestions to the teacher (see Table 6.1).

As in the teacher's manuals, the concern for appropriate text-to-student matching was generally focused on students whose reading abilities were below average. Readability formulas were recommended to be used in selecting easier books. Also as suggested in the manuals, methods books recommended that teachers rewrite portions more simply if the texts were too hard. Seldom were suggestions made about modifying text for students reading above the level of that assigned.

Thus, as in the teacher's manuals, the social studies and science methods textbooks provided some fairly general information on how to estimate difficulty and how to match students and texts. But little of this information seemed specific enough to help teachers judge what was optimal for their students in particular. Teachers were advised to use assigned textbooks as the basic tools for instruction and to simplify the text or select easier materials when the students' reading ability was not up to the level of the standard text. Few suggestions were made for students with higher-than-average reading abilities.

Reading Methods Textbooks

The reading methods textbooks were analyzed separately because reading textbooks present a different problem of matching. The difficulty of reading textbooks is more carefully monitored, and the level of difficulty is indicated on the student textbook. Until a decade or so ago, the designation was the grade in which the text was most commonly used. Most publishers now use consecutive "levels," from 1, for the first preprimer, to about 18, for the sixth-grade reader. It is common practice to use lower-level reading textbooks for students in the higher grades who read below grade level, because the content is not the major consideration in readers, as it is in subject-matter textbooks. Therefore, suitable matching is easier for reading than it is for science and social studies. But there are still important decisions to be made by teachers of reading.

Sample 1: Books Published Between 1950 and 1980.   We analyzed 29 methods textbooks on the teaching of reading, to learn what information they gave to prospective and practicing reading teachers on the issue of text difficulty (see Appendix B-2 for a listing). Almost all of the reading methods textbooks made some reference to text difficulty (refer to Table 6.2) and to how to estimate difficulty by using such procedures as readability formulas, cloze tests, and individualized reading inventories. They also gave suggestions for matching student reading ability to textbook difficulty by grouping students according to their reading abilities and selecting suitable books. Also mentioned, though less frequently than in the manuals and methods textbooks for social studies and science, were suggestions for supplementing the text with easier materials and for rewriting parts of the assigned textbook.

About one-half of the reading methods books addressed optimal difficulty, and more science than social studies methods textbooks did so. One reading methods textbook stressed that books might be too easy, as well as too hard: "If the reading material is too easy, [the student] will be bored and not profit from it: if it is too difficult, he will be frustrated and dislike the task set for him." Another expressed the more frequently found concern that books may be too hard: "Many a teacher . . . has been given books [that are] too difficult for his pupils. . . . Such a situation is too prevalent in public schools and probably one reason why normal development of reading skills is not more commonly achieved." A third recommended that texts be matched not only to reading ability but to other factors: "One of the teacher's functions in teaching comprehension . . . is to select appropriate materials for the students so that there will be a match between the language, content, and cognitive processing demands of the materials and the backgrounds of the students."

Sample 2: Books Published Between 1984 and 1988. We analyzed six widely used reading methods textbooks published between 1984 and 1988 (see Appendix B–2), to compare their treatment of text difficulty with the earlier sample of teacher's manuals and methods textbooks, all of which were published in the early 1980s, prior to the recent concern for more rigorous books found in the media, in reform reports, and in professional journals. More specifically, we wished to learn whether there were changes with regard to the views on the appropriate ease or difficulty of texts, and in the suggestions for assisting students to use textbooks more effectively.

Our analysis of this second sample revealed an even greater concern than in previous years with text difficulty. All of the reading methods texts included suggestions for estimating text difficulty and matching it to student reading achievement. Of particular interest, however, was the use of terms other than *readability* for the same concept. Other terms such as *understandability, usability, interestability,* and *user-friendly* were often used.

For estimating text difficulty, most of the recent reading methods textbooks suggested the use of readability formulas and cloze tests, in which words are systematically deleted and text difficulty is assessed by the number of correct replacements — the more, the easier. Along with these suggestions, however, there were also cautions regarding the limitations of these tools.

Another frequently mentioned recommendation was that texts be evaluated on the broader aspects of the concept of readability, as exemplified in the following statement: "Texts for children should be evaluated on more dimensions than just their readability. They could be analyzed in terms of their literary quality, their interest and appeal to children, or their content." (See Chapter 2 for the historical development of the concept of readability.)

Still another change in the more recently published reading methods textbooks was their greater interest in the use of challenging materials and of textbooks that are of optimal difficulty.

> The concept of readability is important for all teachers. Teachers need to "match" the difficulty level of a book with the instructional level of the student. Students need to function in challenging material that is neither too easy nor too difficult. The closer that match, the better chance for maximum learning to occur. . . .
>   . . . Reading tasks should be at a level of difficulty that maximizes pupils' chance of success, yet not so easy that pupils lose interest.

Finally, as another text warned, "Materials low in challenge may have low appeal."

What is interesting about these statements is their concern for challenge, in terms of both interest and learning:

> Reading materials may be used under a teacher's direction or independently by pupils. Usually the materials in teacher-directed activities can be more difficult than those students use on their own. In either case, the material should be neither so difficult to make learning or enjoyment impossible nor so easy that there is little to learn or to hold the children's interest.

It would appear, overall, that these most current, widely used reading methods textbooks have been responsive to recent criticism of text difficulty. And like the teacher's manuals that accompany reading textbooks, they have tended to use new terms to describe essentially the old and enduring concepts with regard to difficulty of texts and matching textbooks to student reading ability.

SUGGESTIONS FOR EFFECTIVE TEXTBOOK USE IN TEACHER'S MANUALS

To determine what suggestions are given to teachers on helping students to understand their textbooks and to learn from them, we analyzed the social studies and science teacher's manuals on a number of dimensions.

Vocabulary Instruction. All of the social studies and science teacher's manuals gave some attention to vocabulary instruction (see Table 6.3). The most frequent suggestion was to guide students to infer word meanings from context. Previewing of words was also suggested in over half of the manuals, but less than half identified the words to be taught and learned. While only a few of the manuals (12%) specifically recommended tests to check whether the vocabulary had been learned, 38% included such tests. Perhaps their inclusion was considered a tacit recommendation.

Some differences were found by grade level and by content area. Manuals for the fourth-grade texts more often included suggestions for vocabulary instruction than did those for Grades 8 and 11. Social studies manuals gave more attention to vocabulary than the science manuals.

Reading Comprehension Strategies. Table 6.4 shows the extent to which the teacher's manuals focused on reading comprehension in general, and on specific skills or strategies, including reading for main ideas, focusing on details, inferential comprehension, and higher-order (e.g., cause-and-effect, compare/contrast) approaches. We analyzed the manuals to determine what proportion of both the teacher-directed activities they

TABLE 6.3: Percentage of Teacher's Manuals for Social Studies and Science Textbooks Giving Suggestions for Vocabulary Instruction

	Social Studies				Science				All Manuals
	Gr. 4 (*n*=9)	Gr. 8 (*n*=7)	Gr. 11 (*n*=2)	Tot. (*n*=18)	Gr. 4 (*n*=5)	Gr. 8 (*n*=7)	Gr. 11 (*n*=4)	Tot. (*n*=16)	(*N*=34)
Words specified and defined	89	29	0	56	60	0	75	38	47
Previewing suggested	67	71	50	67	60	57	25	50	59
Pronunciation guide provided	78	43	0	56	80	86	50	75	65
Testing suggested	44	0	0	22	0	0	0	0	12
Tests provided	44	29	0	33	20	71	25	44	38
Context suggested	89	57	100	78	80	86	75	81	79

TABLE 6.4: Percentage of Suggested Activities in Teacher's Manuals Giving Attention to Teaching Comprehension

Attention to Skills*	Social Studies ($n = 18$)			Science ($n = 16$)			Total ($N = 34$) Mean
	Teacher-directed	Questions	Mean	Teacher-directed	Questions	Mean	
PARTICULAR SKILLS, ALL GRADES COMBINED							
Main idea	83	67	75	67	40	53	63
Detail	56	61	58	60	40	50	53
Inferential comprehension	78	72	75	60	33	47	60
Higher-order relationships	72	56	64	53	27	40	51
ALL SKILLS COMBINED, BY GRADE							
Fourth	83	72	78	94	63	78	78
Eighth	64	61	63	50	39	45	54
Eleventh	50	38	44	44	0	22	29

*Activities suggested in the introductory section and the section corresponding to the middle chapter of each textbook were analyzed.

suggested and the questions they instructed teachers to ask were designed to foster the development of these four types of comprehension.

Two trends were found. First, attention to comprehension decreased as the grade level increased. Second, in the upper two grades, the social studies manuals gave more attention to comprehension than the science manuals. As can also be seen in Table 6.4, we found that the social studies manuals were substantially more likely to emphasize nonfactual comprehension, such as main idea, inferences, and higher-order relationships, whereas differences between science and social studies manuals with respect to emphasis on factual comprehension (detail) were much smaller. We also found that activities were more frequently suggested than questions in both subject areas and across all grades.

Study Skills Instruction. In analyzing the manuals' emphasis on the teaching of study skills, we distinguished between the simple mention of a skill and practical suggestions for teaching it (see Table 6.5). Differences in study skills by grade tended to be less consistent than differences according to content. Thus the social studies manuals, irrespective of grade, tended to be concerned more with the kinds of study skills necessary for reading and assimilating extensive materials, whereas the science manuals were concerned more with the exacting reading that science requires. More specifically, we found that summarizing is taught more frequently in the social studies manuals and, further, that more attention is paid to this skill as grade level increases — from 33% to 85% to 100% in Grades 4, 8, and 11, respectively. The extent of attention given to summarizing in science manuals remains about the same over the three grades.

TABLE 6.5: Percentage of Teacher's Manuals Mentioning or Providing Study Skills Instruction

| Technique | Social Studies (n = 18) | | | | | | Science (n = 16) | | | | | | All Manuals (N=34) |
| | Gr. 4 (n=9) | | Gr. 8 (n=7) | | Gr. 11 (n=2) | | Gr. 4 (n=5) | | Gr. 8 (n=7) | | Gr. 11 (n=4) | | |
	M[a]	I[b]	M[a]	I[b]	M[a]	I[b]	M[a]	I[b]	M[a]	I[b]	M[a]	I[b]	I[b]
Previewing	56	22	57	14	50	50	60	0	14	43	50	25	24
Adjunct questions	56	33	29	57	50	0	60	0	43	29	25	0	26
Summarizing	33	0	71	14	50	50	60	0	14	43	50	25	18
Skimming/Scanning	56	0	14	0	50	50	0	0	14	0	0	0	3
Outlining	22	0	14	0	50	0	0	0	14	14	0	0	6
Notetaking	22	0	0	0	0	50	0	0	14	43	25	0	12
Writing	44	0	29	14	100	0	0	0	0	14	0	0	6

[a]M = Mentioned.   [b]I = Provided Instruction.

Variations by Student Ability. We also compared the study skills taught in manuals of textbooks that were variously designed by publishers to be "widely used" or to be used with students of higher or lower ability. Generally, manuals for widely used textbooks included more study skills and more practical guidelines for teaching them. Manuals for higher-ability students gave more attention to summarizing and less to previewing, whereas the opposite was true of books for students of lower reading ability.

Use of Graphics. Graphics (charts, graphs, maps, photographs, paintings, drawings, and diagrams) have long been recognized as being related to the readability of instructional materials. As we and others have found, the amount of graphics in textbooks is generally quite considerable (more than one illustration per page) and has been increasing. We therefore sought to learn how the teachers were advised in the manuals to use the graphics. Our findings are presented in Table 6.6. As the table shows, the teacher's manuals tended to classify the graphics by their purpose; that is, whether they were designed to motivate students, focus discussion, stimulate subsequent activity, reinforce information presented in the text, or illustrate such information.

The purpose most frequently stated in both the social studies and science manuals was to use the graphics for illustrating the meaning of ideas presented in the text. Social studies manuals suggested using maps, charts, graphs, and political cartoons to help students grasp and interpret historical trends; the science manuals indicated that graphics could help clarify the directions for laboratory experiments, which also falls in the category of illustrating meaning. The second most frequent suggestion was for the use of illustrations to reinforce information presented in the text discourse.

TABLE 6.6: **Percentage of Teacher's Manuals Giving Attention to the Use of Graphics and Follow-Up Activities**

| Purpose | Social Studies | | | | Science | | | | All Manuals |
| | Gr. 4 | Gr. 8 | Gr. 11 | Total | Gr. 4 | Gr. 8 | Gr. 11 | Total | |
	(*n*=9)	(*n*=7)	(*n*=2)	(*n*=18)	(*n*=5)	(*n*=7)	(*n*=4)	(*n*=16)	(*N*=34)
GRAPHICS									
Illustrate meaning given in text	78	43	0	55	80	57	50	63	59
Reinforce information given in text	78	29	0	50	80	57	0	50	50
Motivation	56	0	0	27	40	57	0	33	32
Focus for discussion	56	14	0	33	60	14	0	22	29
Stimulate follow-up activities	22	14	0	17	20	43	0	22	21
FOLLOW-UP ACTIVITIES									
Additional sources of information	33	29	100	39	80	57	75	69	53
Encourage reading	89	71	50	78	80	43	0	44	62

Motivation was the third most frequently mentioned purpose found for the graphics, with about one-third offering this suggestion. For example, a fourth-grade social studies manual suggested that a picture of Mt. St. Helens be used to introduce a study of the Northwest, and an eighth-grade social studies manual recommended using maps of railway systems in the early 1900s and the present to encourage comparison by students of these time periods.

Focusing discussion with the use of graphics was suggested in over one-quarter of the manuals. One of the science manuals recommended using a picture of a light circuit to initiate a discussion of electricity, and a history manual suggested that studying photographs of a particular era might provide evidence of that culture's customs and attitudes.

Suggestions for using graphics as stimuli for subsequent activities were the least common, although they did appear in over one-fifth of the manuals.

Follow-up Activities. Table 6.6 also shows the percentage of various follow-up activities suggested. About half of the manuals provided lists of books and audiovisual materials for students pursuing individual topics, and nearly two-thirds suggested activities for encouraging reading. The latter included making a labeled diagram of objects associated with electrical wiring, collecting pictures illustrating the Northeast and translating them into a map, and doing independent research in order to make a diagram of how a canal works.

Writing. We examined the teacher's manuals to see how many of them included suggestions related to developing students' writing abilities; our results are given in Table 6.5 (above). As can be seen, very little attention was given to writing in the manuals, particularly when it came to providing instruction. While writing was at least mentioned in about 40% of the social studies manuals, it was addressed in only 7% of the science manuals. Actual instruction for written activities was given only in the eighth-grade manuals, and only in 14% of them. The writing that was suggested was designed to "encourage students to write full sentences rather than just letters, checks, or other symbols of objective questions." Other writing suggestions included asking students to write an essay on "Invention and American Society in the Nineteenth Century." However, most of the manuals addressed writing through such general statements as the following: "As students prepare library reports and answer review questions, they practice writing skills."

Our visits to science classes, however, revealed that some teachers do assign considerably more writing than their manuals seem to suggest, but it is generally of the kind needed for keeping notebooks and records of laboratory work (see Chapter 7). Overall, the manuals' concern with writing seems not to have advanced much from our findings of over a decade ago (Chall et al., 1977), when most textbooks paid little or no attention to writing.

SUMMARY AND CONCLUSIONS

Our purpose in analyzing teacher's manuals and books on teaching methods was twofold. First, we sought to learn how publishers and authors of methods textbooks informed teachers about text difficulty and the procedures they might use for matching texts and students. Second, we wished to learn how the teacher's manuals assisted teachers in helping students to learn from texts and to improve their reading strategies and study skills.

Overall, the teacher's manuals and the methods texts for social studies and science did pay attention to issues of text difficulty and to ways of effecting a suitable match with student ability. More than half also suggested ways in which teachers might assess text difficulty and match it to students' reading abilities. But neither the extent nor the kind of information about difficulty presented to teachers of social studies and science was consistent with the strong concern for text difficulty expressed by teachers and publishers in our surveys (see Chapters 3 and 4). The information on text difficulty given in the teacher's manuals and methods textbooks was sparse and tended to lack specificity. Further, it included little information on what constituted an optimal match.

More of the books on methods of teaching reading were concerned with text difficulty, although they paid somewhat less attention than content methods books to ways of matching textbooks to students' reading abilities. Most of the reading methods books presented specific information on how to assess difficulty, such as by the use of readability formulas, cloze tests, and individualized reading inventories. More of them also suggested ways to effect a suitable match of text to student, mostly by reading ability grouping. Like the social studies and science manuals and methods textbooks, the reading methods texts were concerned mainly with finding suitable texts for below-average readers; little concern was expressed that textbooks might be unsuitable for students because they were too easy.

An analysis of newer reading methods texts published from 1984 to 1988 revealed a greater concern for difficulty and for matching texts to student reading achievement. They suggested and gave specific instructions for using a variety of techniques. There was a growing tendency to cite the limitations of readability formulas, although their use was suggested as one procedure available to teachers. More than in the earlier methods textbooks, additional terms were used synonymously with *readability*, such as *understandability, usability, interestability*, and *considerate texts*. This is also the trend in current teacher's manuals. The newer reading methods texts also showed greater concern than those of the early 1980s for using "challenging" texts, which are neither too difficult nor too easy.

Our second set of questions addressed the kind of guidance and strategies publishers gave teachers for enhancing student learning from textbooks. Since the amount and kind of guidance given by teachers can help students to learn, particularly from harder texts, the guidance provided in teacher's manuals is also a factor in a text's difficulty. The more students are helped to learn from their texts, the more difficult the text can be. For this purpose, we focused on the areas of assistance given in vocabulary, comprehension, study skills, the use of graphics, and writing.

Most manuals paid more attention to comprehension than to vocabulary. With regard to vocabulary, more attention was paid to vocabulary in in the elementary grades than in high school.

Most of the manuals suggested that teachers encourage students to get meanings of unknown words by using the context. Many of the manuals also recommended previewing difficult words and using pronunciation guides in dictionaries, but only a few identified the particular words to be previewed or indicated which words might require the use of pronunciation guides. Also, few of the manuals recommended testing the students' learning of the words taught or provided guidelines for designing such tests.

The manuals gave considerable attention to comprehension strategies. Both social studies and science manuals addressed the need to teach a variety of comprehension strategies for both literal and inferential levels of understanding. Overall, social studies manuals gave more instruction for teaching comprehension, particularly the nonliteral aspects. This attention to broader comprehension strategies is no doubt related to the greater need for inferential thinking in social studies and the greater need for attention to specific technical knowledge in science.

As with teaching vocabulary, the amount of attention given to comprehension strategies decreased with increasing grade. It would seem that, the more it was needed, the less it was provided.

Study skills coverage in the teacher's manuals exhibited no notable trends. Overall, study skills were mentioned more often than directions for teaching them. The social studies manuals generally gave more attention to study skills than did the science manuals, which was similar to our findings for vocabulary and reading comprehension.

Suggestions for writing appeared relatively infrequently in both the social studies and science manuals, but more frequently in those for social studies. This trend was similar to what we found in our study in 1977 (Chall et al., 1977).

CHAPTER 7

Uses of Textbooks in Classrooms

This chapter addresses classroom uses of textbooks. Specifically, we wanted to know how teachers selected textbooks that were appropriate for their students; whether the grades they taught, the subject matter, and the reading abilities of their students influenced their choices; and how the textbooks were used in the classroom.

We observed lessons in over 27 elementary classrooms (9 each in fourth-, sixth-, and eighth-grades) and 18 eleventh-grade classrooms in three school systems representing high, high-average, and low-average reading achievement — nearly 100 observations in all. (It should be noted that the elementary schools in our study were all K–8, and we have therefore included eighth grade within our analysis and discussion of elementary schools.) We also analyzed the readability of the textbooks used most often in the classrooms, as well as that of other instructional materials (unpublished and/or prepublished) used by some of the teachers. A complete listing of all the materials analyzed is given in Appendix B–4; for ease of discussion, we will refer to all of these as textbooks in the following analysis. Many of the textbooks in this sample also appeared in our general sample of textbooks analyzed in Chapter 5.

READING DIFFICULTY
OF ELEMENTARY TEXTBOOKS

The difficulty levels of the 75 instructional materials used for science, social studies, and reading in fourth, sixth, and eighth grades were quite similar to the levels found in the larger sample of books analyzed in Chapter 5. The readability scores of most of the content-area books used in the classes were generally above the grade level for which they were intended. As can be seen in Table 7.1, all fourth-grade social studies and science books were at least one grade band above fourth grade, and in the sixth-

TABLE 7.1 Readability Scores of Text Materials Used in Fourth-, Sixth-, and Eighth-Grade Classrooms

GRADE/SUBJECT/Ability Designation	Number of books	Mean Readability score of book(s)*
FOURTH GRADE (N = 25 books)		
SOCIAL STUDIES (n = 5 books)		
Mixed	1	5-6
Mixed	1	5-6
Mixed	3	5-6
SCIENCE (n = 6 books)		
Mixed	2	5-6
Mixed	1	5-6
Mixed	3	7-8
READING (n = 14 books)		
Below Average	2	2
Below Average	1	3
Below Average	1	3
Average and Below Average	1	4
Average	1	2
Average	1	4
Average and Above Average	1	3
Average and Above Average	1	4
Average and Above Average	2	5-6
Above Average	1	4
Above Average	1	4
Above Average	1	5-6
SIXTH GRADE (N = 27 books)		
SOCIAL STUDIES (n = 6 books)		
Mixed	1	5-6
Mixed	1	7-8
Mixed	1	7-8
Average and Below Average	1	5-6
Average	2	7-8
SCIENCE (n = 7 books)		
Mixed	2	5-6
SIXTH GRADE, SCIENCE (continued)		
Mixed	2	7-8
Below Average	1	7-8
Average	1	11-12
Above Average	1	5-6
READING (n = 14 books)		
Mixed	4	5-6
Below Average	1	5-6
Below Average	4	5-6
Average	1	5-6
Average	1	7-8
Average and Above Average	1	5-6
Above Average	1	5-6
Above Average	1	7-8
EIGHTH GRADE (N = 23 books)		
SOCIAL STUDIES (n = 7 books)		
Mixed	1	9-10
Mixed	1	9-10
Average and Below Average	3	7-8
Average and Above Average	1	9-10
Above Average	1	9-10
SCIENCE (n = 6 books)		
Mixed	1	9-10
Mixed	1	7-8
Mixed	3	9-10
Above Average	1	11-12
READING (n = 10 books)		
Mixed	1	5-6
Mixed	4	5-6
Mixed	2	7-8
Average and Below Average	3	5-6

*Books were analyzed with the Spache and Dale-Chall formulas and the Fry graph.

grade classes, only 40 % of the content-area books used were on grade level (5–6), while 60 % scored in the next level up or higher. In these grades there seemed to be little or no association between the difficulty level of the book and the average reading ability of the students in the class in which it was used: Classes composed of average and below-average readers might well be using social studies and science books that were more difficult than those used in classes composed of students whose abilities were above average. In the eighth-grade classes, only two of the social studies and science books were on grade level (7–8), and all of the rest were above grade level; there was a tendency, however, for the easier books to be used in classes of average and below-average reading ability, and the hardest to be used in above-average classes.

Our findings for the reading textbooks used in fourth-, sixth-, and eighth-grade classrooms were somewhat different. For almost all classes, the reading textbooks were easier than those for social studies and science; half were on grade level, and over a third were below. The few books that scored above grade level were never more than one band above the grade. As can be seen in Table 7.1, there was a tendency for the difficulty of the text to be related to reading ability of the class for the fourth-grade classes, but no such pattern could be found in the other two grades.

Our analysis of books used in classrooms thus showed that content-area textbooks were generally harder than reading textbooks and that the selection of easier or harder books was not consistently associated with the reading ability designation of these classes.

MATCH BETWEEN READING DIFFICULTY OF ELEMENTARY TEXTBOOKS AND STUDENTS' READING ACHIEVEMENT LEVELS

For a more precise evaluation of the difficulty of the textbooks for fourth-, sixth-, and eighth-grade students, we compared the readability scores of the books to students' reading achievement levels. The standardized reading test scores of 54 students in each grade were used together with teachers' estimates of their performance (whether they were above-average, average, or below-average readers) as a measure of students' reading achievement levels.

Table 7.2 shows the relationship between these reading achievement levels and the readability scores of the books used most often in the social studies, science, and reading classes. The findings are quite similar to the more general comparison of books and grade levels shown in Table 7.1. That is, most reading textbooks were equal to or below students' reading achievement, just as the readability scores of most reading books were on or below grade placement. In contrast, most science and social studies

TABLE 7.2: Relationship Between Students' Standardized Reading Test Scores and the Readability Levels of Their Primary Text Materials

	Relation of Materials' Readability Scores to Students' Standardized Reading Test Scores		
GRADE/Subject	Below Students' Scores	Equal to Students' Scores	Above Students' Scores
FOURTH GRADE			
Social studies	22	41	37
Science	0	52	48
Reading	67	33	0
SIXTH GRADE			
Social studies	22	43	35
Science	19	37	44
Reading	32	61	7
EIGHTH GRADE			
Social studies	2	52	46
Science	4	39	57
Reading	59	41	0

books were equal to or above students' reading achievement levels, just as they were on or above grade placement in readability.

READING DIFFICULTY OF HIGH SCHOOL TEXTBOOKS

We extended our observations beyond elementary classrooms, to eleventh-grade science and social studies classes, in order to learn whether the trends we found in the lower grades continued. We observed 18 classes and analyzed the major textbook used in each. These classes were identified as above average, average, or below average, and students were assigned to them primarily on the basis of their standardized test scores.

Table 7.3 presents the mean readability scores of the textbooks used most often in each of these classes. Overall, slightly less than half of the social studies books were on grade level and slightly more than half below, ranging from a fifth- to a twelfth-grade level. The books used in below-average classes were generally below grade level and easier than those used in above-average classes, which were on grade level.

In science classes, five of the nine books were above grade level (16 +), two were on grade level (11–12), and two were below (9–10). The easiest of the science books were used in below-average classes, but the harder books were used more often in average than in above-average classes.

The greater difficulty of the textbooks in high school science classes was generally consistent with that found for the elementary grades. Elev-

TABLE 7.3: Readability Scores of Eleventh-Grade Social Studies and Science Textbooks ($N = 18$)

Classes	Subjects	
	Social Studies	Science
Average	7-8	16+
	9-10	16+
	11-12	16+
Below Average	5-6	9-10
	9-10	16+
	9-10	9-10
Above Average	11-12	16+
	11-12	11-12
	11-12	11-12

enth-grade social studies books, however, ran counter to our results for the earlier grades, where we found many above-grade-level books, particularly for the fourth grade. None of the eleventh-grade social studies books were above grade level in difficulty.

In the earlier grades, the difficulty levels of the books used seemed to have little relationship to the students' reading achievement levels. In high school classes, there seems to be some association of text difficulty with students' reading achievement, although here, too, it was a less-than-consistent relationship.

INSTRUCTIONAL APPROACHES TO TEXTBOOK USE

In the latter half of this chapter, we describe the various ways that we saw textbooks being used in classroom settings. Our observations will be given separately for elementary and high school levels, but first we will discuss three relatively distinct patterns or approaches that emerged and could be found to varying degrees at both levels. The differences that distinguish these approaches from each other occur in the emphasis placed on the use of the textbook and in the amount and kind of guidance given by the teacher before, during, and after reading. The three approaches are:

1. *Directed-Lesson Approach.* This pattern was characterized by a teacher who carefully and explicitly guided students' reading throughout a lesson. Before they read, the teacher reviewed or taught the meanings of new or unfamiliar words and asked questions to help students relate their previous knowledge to the lesson's topic. During the reading, the teacher

asked questions and elicited explanations of information and concepts presented in the book. After reading, the teacher helped students summarize their reading and asked more questions, to review what had been learned.

2. *Study-Skills Approach.* Assistance was provided by the teacher in gathering and organizing information from the textbook. The teacher did not directly guide students' reading, but asked leading questions and previewed vocabulary before the book was read. Study guides were often provided, usually in the form of work sheets for students to use while they read. Following reading, the teacher showed students how to clarify and order the information they had read, by outlining, summarizing, and the like. The amount of instruction given by teachers using this pattern varied according to students' reading abilities and their ability to work with minimal direction. Often the lesson was discussed in class, but completed as homework, with the textbook being a major learning resource.

3. *Multiple-Resource Approach.* Teachers whose use of textbooks suggested this pattern did not rely on them as the primary instructional tool. They used a variety of resources — lectures, discussions, audiovisual media, and hands-on experiences — in addition to textbooks. Selections from textbooks were usually assigned as homework and then discussed in class. The teacher's questions were commonly designed to check on what had been learned, rather than to guide the learning (see Durkin, 1978–1979).

These three patterns seemed to be related to the subjects and the grades taught. Generally, the lower the grades, the more often the teachers used the directed lessons. The higher the grades, the more they used the study-skills and multiple-resource approaches.

HOW TEXTBOOKS WERE USED IN ELEMENTARY CLASSROOMS

In the following pages, we describe what we learned from observing the use of textbooks in elementary classrooms. We begin with comments on organization of the classes and descriptions of general patterns of teaching behavior. From these, we move to more specific observations about how textbooks were used for social studies, science, and reading.

General Observations

It will come as no surprise to any observer of schools that the elementary classes we visited differed in composition and in instructional grouping. Fourth-grade classes were usually self-contained; eighth-grade classes were departmentalized. Sixth-grade classes varied between the two. Whole-class instruction was given in all social studies and science classes, but the organization of the reading classes differed by grade. In fourth-grade class-rooms, reading was usually taught in three groups, organized according to reading achievement; in sixth- and eighth-grade classes, most reading instruction was given to an entire class. The exception was sixth-grade classes in the low-average school system, where students were grouped by reading achievement.

The organization of the classes affected the amount of time spent on each subject. In departmentalized classes, prearranged schedules allowed approximately 40 minutes for each subject. In self-contained classes, reading classes averaged about 50 minutes per day (250 minutes per week); social studies and science, about 35 (175 minutes per week).

Textbooks were used in almost all the classes we observed. The few classes in which textbooks were not used were science classes where experiments, lectures, and visual aids predominated. One book or one set of materials was the norm in most science and social studies classes; in reading classes, a variety of materials were assigned, usually according to the students' reading abilities.

Almost twice as many pages were covered in the reading lessons we observed as in the social studies and science lessons. This difference was no doubt influenced by the differences in time allotted to each class and by the difficulty of the textbooks.

In the fourth- and sixth-grade classes we observed a strong reliance on teacher's manuals in all three subjects. In the eighth-grade classes they were used less frequently.

Social Studies Classes

The most frequently observed patterns in elementary social studies classes were the directed-lesson and multiple-resource approaches. The former was used in most fourth-grade classes and in sixth-grade below-average classes. Teachers asked more questions before assigning the reading lesson than during or after. The majority of questions were aimed at relating students' knowledge to ideas to be read. Questions following the reading were often about facts within the text, and students were encouraged to "look back" for answers.

The multiple-resource approach was observed in most of the sixth-grade social studies classes. Teachers relied more on discussions, visual aids, and simulations of historical events than on textbooks, which were assigned for homework with little or no preparatory direction. New vocabulary was discussed after the book was read and was more often tested than taught. In these classes, teaching seemed to stress the acquisition of a body of knowledge or a set of concepts. We noticed that questions asked in these classes seemed to call not only for the recall of facts but for explanation, integration, and application of knowledge.

The study-skills pattern was observed in most eighth-grade social studies classes. Teachers guided their students in the use of organizational aids such as chapter headings and subheadings, topic sentences, and text summaries. They defined and discussed new and unfamiliar vocabulary. After independent reading, they led the class in discussions and demonstrated models for organizing related information, outlining, and note taking.

Science Classes

The directed-lesson approach was observed in elementary science classes at all three grade levels, but particularly in fourth and sixth grades. Demonstration of experiments often preceded assigned reading, as did questions intended to elicit facts and clarify prior knowledge. Teachers introduced unfamiliar vocabulary and interspersed questions throughout the reading, to encourage students' understanding and integration of ideas.

Some science teachers used aspects of both the directed-lesson and study-skills approaches. They encouraged their students to search for information by reading specific textbook passages and demonstrated procedures for extracting relevant information.

Experiments and textbook reading were also often combined in science classes where the study-skills pattern was observed. About half of the eighth-grade science teachers used their textbook as a laboratory manual, guiding students through an organized sequence of tasks: first reading the book to see what to do, then gathering materials, and finally reviewing the book for directions. This pattern was used as often in below-average eighth-grade classes as in above-average ones.

Science teachers who followed a multiple-resource approach emphasized scientific thought and experimentation, with limited reference to the textbook. These teachers expected a great deal of writing and note taking from their students. In one fourth-grade class, students worked individually, drawing and labeling microscopic plant and animal life. Their teacher explained, "A lot of concepts in science come from doing and seeing. Teaching science is to arouse interest and practice study skills." In a sixth-grade science class in the same school system, students drew and labeled parts of disassembled batteries and made charts and notes to accompany their experiments with light bulbs and batteries. By the time students in this system were in eighth-grade science classes, they were expected to write descriptive answers to guided questions and to take detailed notes of lectures, experiments, and discussions.

Reading Classes

The directed-lesson pattern was observed in almost all elementary reading classes — all fourth-grade classes and many sixth- and eighth-grade classes. Reading teachers made the most frequent use of manuals. They taught vocabulary before assigning the reading selections, and, as their students read, they stopped them periodically to ask questions, discuss main ideas, or review vocabulary in context. Stories in the reading textbooks were almost always read more than once, first silently, then orally. In most classes, students also used workbooks and teacher-made work sheets.

One eighth-grade teacher said she preferred the directed-lesson approach because "it helped students become more active readers." Another eighth-grade teacher explained, "This is the students' last opportunity for guided reading. After this they will be on their own. They need to know how to deal with challenging materials."

The study-skills pattern was observed in fewer reading than social studies and science classes. Generally, in the upper elementary grades, classes of lower achievers or of mixed reading abilities used reading laboratories, which were sets of reading tasks graded by difficulty. These students generally worked independently, following the directions that accompanied the materials, but the teacher was available for guidance when needed.

The multiple-resource pattern was observed in several sixth-grade reading classes composed of above-average students. It was preferred by a former English teacher and a science teacher who were both assigned to teach reading. The first teacher assigned the textbook for homework and then led seminar-type discussions of the ideas and literary qualities of the selections, probing for ideas on plot, setting, character, and theme. Essay writing was also emphasized. The former science teacher taught the process of getting information from a story. Although vocabulary and study skills were not addressed prior to the reading, concepts related to the reading selection were explained and amplified in the discussions. This teacher expressed a preference for teaching reading with a science or social studies book rather than with a reading book. "Reading textbooks just put people to sleep," he commented.

HOW TEXTBOOKS WERE USED IN HIGH SCHOOL CLASSROOMS

In the 18 eleventh-grade classes we observed, all of the social studies teachers and most of the science teachers said that textbooks served as their primary instructional tools. However, the manner and extent of their use of textbooks varied in ways that paralleled our observations of elementary classrooms; for example, the more advanced the students, the more the multiple-resource and study-skills patterns were used.

Social Studies Classes

The multiple-resource pattern was observed most frequently in all classes. It was characterized by a minimum of prereading instruction; the assignment of independent reading; and extensive use of lectures, discussions, and audiovisual materials. This pattern was seen most often in above-average classes. In one, lectures and discussions were used to review and supplement homework reading assignments. In another, a variety of sources were used as the basis for a seminar-type discussion, with individual students contributing significant information from their independent research. The teacher asked questions that required students to abstract, synthesize, and evaluate materials read. In a third above-average class, the teacher introduced a new unit with a discussion of vocabulary: *humanism, individualism, secularism, Renaissance person.* He guided students in exploring these concepts, asking them, for example, to think of someone they might consider a Renaissance person today. Following this exercise, a videotape on the Renaissance was shown, during which the teacher stopped the videotape from time to time to discuss key concepts and vocabulary.

Some teachers in average-ability classes also followed the multiple-resource pattern. In a typical class, writing assignments were based on independent reading, as were such assignments as answering questions that required the evaluation and integration of ideas (e.g., "What is your opinion of Rockefeller's and Carnegie's explanation of business success?"). Discussions of these questions were followed by a filmstrip on the history of regulatory agencies that required a solid grasp of the interplay of events and a familiarity with such historical figures as Rockefeller and Gould. The teacher encouraged a variety of perspectives and helped students with difficult material through oral reading from the textbook and other sources.

Some of the teachers of below-average high school classes also used the multiple-resource pattern, relying less on print materials and more on lectures and visual aids. In one class, lectures were supplemented by slides of historical maps, graphs, and charts. Another used a combination of reading in the text and discussions, which encouraged students to personalize history through comparing "then" and "now."

In the remainder of the social studies classes, we observed a modified version of the directed-lesson pattern. Teachers prepared students for reading by previewing new vocabulary and discussing key concepts. Average and above-average classes pursued independent reading and writing activities, while in the below-average class, students worked with close supervision and assistance from the teacher. Homework, which generally involved the preparation of questions to be discussed in class, was modeled by the teacher.

Science Classes

In eleventh-grade science classes, most teachers used a combined form of the multiple-resources and study-skills patterns. Typically they introduced specific concepts and provided a general framework or goal before assigning reading. They required students to relate their laboratory work to concepts presented in their textbooks and other materials. Students were often taught to take notes on their laboratory experiments and reading assignments. Laboratory experiences were consistently integrated into class discussions, lectures, and reading from the text. In one class, for example, the teacher conducted a demonstration of atmospheric pressure. Students took notes and then read an explanation of the experiment, to verify what they had just observed. Science textbooks seemed to be used more in average eleventh-grade classes and less in above-average and below-average classes. When students could not read the text, teachers used oral presentations, demonstrations, and student-conducted experiments for disseminating information.

In summary, although most science teachers provided some assistance, direct instruction in using textbooks was not the general rule. Priority was given to learning subject-specific concepts in almost all the classes, and a variety of learning experiences were employed. Textbooks were emphasized most in average classes and least in classes for above- or below-average students.

SUMMARY AND CONCLUSIONS

Textbooks served as the primary instructional tool in the majority of the classrooms we observed. The practice of using a single textbook was found in both the elementary and high schools, although secondary teachers were more likely to use supplementary materials as well as texts. In the elementary classrooms, textbooks were used most often in reading classes. In high school, where reading is no longer taught as a separate subject, about the same amount of time was spent with textbooks in social studies and science classrooms.

The most pronounced differences between elementary and secondary classes were in the way textbooks were used. Elementary teachers used textbooks to develop reading skills as well as to teach content in reading, social studies, and science classes. Most of the teachers used a directed-lesson pattern in which they devoted considerable instruction to how to read and gather information from textbooks. This practice was observed more in fourth and sixth than in eighth grades, but also in average and below-average classes in the eighth grade. Teachers of eighth-grade classes and of more able readers in the two lower grades generally followed a study-skills approach for teaching social studies and science, encouraging students to extract information by identifying organizational features of the textbook. Some social studies and science teachers emphasized the learning of content and followed a multiple-resource pattern in which films, lectures, discussion, and the textbook were all considered important. This pattern was found primarily in above-average and below-average classrooms. Students who found the textbook too difficult were expected to learn the material through these other means.

At the eleventh-grade level, we found relatively little use of the directed-lesson pattern. The focus was mainly on learning content. Generally, social studies teachers assigned reading prior to questions and discussions, whereas in science classes reading usually followed these activities. However, both groups put rather limited emphasis on the process of learning from textbooks, focusing more on what was to be learned — the content. Such a focus is not unexpected, since, by the time they reach secondary school, even below-average students are expected to have some experience and skill in learning from textbooks.

Although detailed studies of the use of textbooks in actual classrooms are relatively rare, our findings regarding the differential use of textbooks seem fairly consistent with those studies that have addressed similar issues. Freeman and Porter (1988), for example, found wide variation in elementary math teachers' use of their textbooks, in terms of what content was covered, how much was covered, and in what sequence. Using teachers' self-reports and interviews, the researchers identified several "styles" of textbook use that ranged from almost total reliance to a fairly independent stance.

Stodolsky's (1989) observations of instructional activities in elementary math and social studies classrooms also revealed a range of "postures" with regard to how teachers — in this case all were experienced teachers — used their textbooks and teacher's guidebooks. Among the various styles described by Stodolsky was one that adhered strictly to the manual — similar to our directed-reading pattern — and a second one described as we did — a multiple-resource pattern.

Stodolsky (1989) suggested that differences in subject matter as well as the nature of the texts might be related to the variations she observed. We would agree with this conclusion and add that grade level and the relationship between students' reading abilities and text difficulty may also be influential factors in the way teachers use textbooks.

CHAPTER 8

Students and Their Textbooks

In discussions of textbooks, students are often considered the forgotten constituency (e.g., Tyson-Bernstein, 1988b). They have little to say about their books, what they should include, and how they should be written. Such decisions are made for them, albeit in the name of their best interests. This chapter concentrates on students. It is concerned with how well they understand the books they use and what they think about the way they are written. Altogether, 213 students participated in this part of the study— 162 elementary students and 51 high school students. (Procedures for student testing and interviews are given in Appendix C–1.)

STUDENT READING ABILITY
AND LEVEL OF COMPREHENSION

Our first concern was whether students could read and comprehend the books they were using. To assess comprehension, we administered cloze tests (see Appendix C–2) developed from their reading, social studies, and science books. To construct the cloze tests, we deleted every tenth word from passages taken from the various books. Students replaced the deleted words, and their cloze scores were the percentage of exact replacements.

Cloze tests were one of five types of tests, including recall and oral reading, that we initially piloted. Since all were highly correlated with one another and with students' standardized test scores, we used the cloze test because it was the easiest and most objective to construct, administer, and score.

A cloze score of approximately 40% has been found to equal about 75% correct on multiple-choice tests, a level considered to represent adequate understanding (Bormuth, 1967). A range of cloze scores, usually from 35% to 45%, is most commonly used. Following this precedent, we selected 35% as our index of adequate comprehension; students who scored at or above this level on the cloze tests were considered to have adequate comprehension, while the comprehension of those who scored lower was considered to be less than adequate.

Passages for the test were taken from the main textbooks used by the students. The readability of these books had already been determined (see Chapter 7, especially Tables 7.1 and 7.3).* We selected from each book two passages whose readability scores were consistent with those of the book as a whole; each passage contained a coherent idea or sequence of thought. One passage served as the cloze instrument, and the other was used as the stimulus for eliciting students' judgments about their textbooks.

Our results for these cloze tests are given in Table 8.1. They indicate that, for most grades and subjects, the better the readers (on standardized tests), the better they understood their books (on the cloze tests).

Fourth-grade students found their reading textbooks relatively easier to understand than their social studies or science books; most students reached an adequate comprehension level on their reading cloze tests. Most

TABLE 8.1: Percentage of Students Achieving an Adequate Comprehension Score on Social Studies, Science, and Reading Passages ($N = 213$)

	Percentage Achieving Adequate Score		
	Social Studies	Science	Reading
FOURTH GRADE ($n = 54$)			
Below average ($n = 3$)	0	0	0
Average ($n = 23$)	26	39	65
Above average ($n = 28$)	79	75	79
SIXTH GRADE ($n = 54$)			
Below average ($n = 6$)	17	67	33
Average ($n = 19$)	26	47	42
Above average ($n = 29$)	62	90	97
EIGHTH GRADE ($n = 54$)			
Below average ($n = 1$)	0	0	0
Average ($n = 35$)	57	51	34
Above average ($n = 18$)	94	94	89
ELEVENTH GRADE ($n = 51$)			
Below average ($n = 10$)	40	50	——*
Average ($n = 23$)	87	83	——*
Above average ($n = 18$)	100	100	——*

*Since eleventh graders were not taught reading, this comparison did not apply.

---

*The majority of reading textbooks had readabilities either equal to or lower than the students' reading achievement scores. Elementary social studies and science books were harder, scoring either at or above student reading levels. In high school, social studies books were generally at the students' grade level or below, while science books were at grade level or above.

of the above-average students also reached an adequate comprehension level on their social studies and science books, but fewer than one-third of all average and below-average students did. Thus the cloze scores seemed also to be related to the difficulty of the books; that is, the reading textbooks, which had easier readability scores than the other books, produced higher cloze-test scores.

Patterns of sixth-grade cloze scores were essentially the same as for the fourth graders. Sixth-grade students' achievement scores, their cloze comprehension scores, and the readability of their textbook were positively related: The higher their standardized reading test scores, the higher their comprehension of their textbooks; and the lower the readability scores of the passages, the higher the cloze comprehension. Of particular note here was the 67% of below-average students who did well on the science passages, twice as many as those who scored adequately on the reading passages, which were easier. We will return to this later in our discussion.

Our findings for the eighth grade were similar to those for the lower two grades: The higher their general reading ability, the better students comprehended their textbooks. Of special interest here was the somewhat higher percentage of average students who achieved an adequate score on the social studies and science passages. Once again, below-average readers had the most difficulty with all the books.

Eleventh-grade scores followed the same pattern as those of elementary-grade students, in terms of the positive relationship between reading achievement and cloze scores. The relationship of cloze comprehension to readability level was, however, not as consistent. Students' scores were fairly similar on both science and social studies books, even though the science books had considerably higher readability scores.

In summary, the results of cloze testing suggested that most students in all elementary classrooms understood their reading textbooks. Between 62% and 100% of the above-average students in all four grades understood their social studies books, but these books were understood by fewer average readers—between 26% and 88%. As grade level increased, greater percentages of students could adequately comprehend their content textbooks.

The below-average readers consistently had the most difficulty understanding their textbooks. The single exception was the 67% of below-average sixth graders who had adequate comprehension of the science passages—the figure is higher even than that for average readers. While we cannot fully explain this, it is interesting to note that this high percentage occurred in science, rather than in social studies and reading, even though the readability level of some of the science books was higher. This may be related to the structure of the writing in science books, where the style tends to be straightforward, well-ordered, and often redundant in the repetition of technical words. Such writing may well be related to higher cloze scores and, as our stage analysis of the eighth- and eleventh-grade science books indicated, to a level of conceptual difficulty lower than the readability scores would suggest (see Tables 5.5 and 5.8).

These findings are of interest for several reasons. First, although the educational literature has, for several years, been critical of standardized reading tests and of readability measurement, our findings support their usefulness. In the present study, both measures were able to predict students' ability to comprehend texts. (See Fry, 1989, for additional support.) Second, independently administered cloze tests tended to confirm the predictions of the readability measures and the reading comprehension scores.

Thus it would appear that the concern for appropriate difficulty of textbooks expressed by publishers, teachers, and textbook-adoption committees in our surveys is a legitimate concern. Difficulty does seem to make a difference in how much students understand and learn from their textbooks. Indeed, the NAEP found it to be of primary importance in the understanding of text: "Basically, analyses of the NAEP data indicate that the interaction of three factors affects students' reading proficiency: the complexity of the material they were asked to read, their familiarity with the subject matter, and the kinds of questions asked" (NAEP, 1985, p. 14). Thus, it would seem that although newer and better instruments for measuring the complexity of materials are always to be sought and welcomed, those that exist can be used constructively to match students and texts.

STUDENT JUDGMENTS OF TEXTBOOKS AND PREFERENCES FOR DIFFICULTY

This section reports on the judgments of students about the difficulty of their textbooks, as well as describing their preferences. They were asked if their books were too easy, too hard, or just about right; and how hard their ideal book would be. We asked students for these judgments and preferences in terms of a typical passage from the textbooks they were using. (The instrument used for these interviews is given in Appendix C–3.)

Students' judgments were analyzed according to their cloze scores and to the difficulty of the passage they were reading. Overall, however, their judgments did not vary consistently with either. The largest percentage — about two-thirds — rated the passage they had read as being just about right for them.

Were the approximately one-third of the students who rated their books too easy or too hard influenced by their cloze scores or the text difficulty? We examined the judgments of all groups according to grade and subject and chose the 16 with the largest percentages of "too easy" or "too hard" ratings. Table 8.2 presents these groups, their grade levels, and their judgments of their books. It shows their test scores and the difficulty of their books. This comparison suggests students' judgments may be related to both their understanding of the passage (as demonstrated by their cloze scores) and the level of passage difficulty (as demonstrated by the readability level of the textbook), at least when they thought the passages were too hard or too easy.

In general, students with inadequate cloze comprehension scores were more likely to rate passages "too hard"; furthermore, those passages rated "too hard" were more likely to have readability scores above grade level. In contrast, students with adequate comprehension were more likely to rate passages as "too easy," and the readability of the passages so rated was more likely to be on or below grade level in difficulty.

Overall, our study of students' judgments of difficulty suggests they are reasonably astute about the textbooks they read. They know with a fairly high degree of accuracy which are too easy, which are too hard, and which are just about right, and these judgments seem to correlate fairly closely

TABLE 8.2: **Groups of Students, by Subject and Grade, in Which the Largest Percentage Rated Their Book Too Easy or Too Hard**

Group's Judgment/ Subject of Text	Grade	% Judging Too Hard or Too Easy	Students' Cloze Test Scores	Readability Level of Textbook
JUDGMENTS OF TOO HARD				
Reading	6	29	Inadequate	On Grade
Reading	8	53	Inadequate	On Grade
Social studies	4	31	Adequate	Above Grade
Social studies	4	33	Inadequate	Above Grade
Social studies	6	33	Inadequate	Above Grade
Social studies	8	29	Inadequate	Above Grade
Science	11	67	Inadequate	Above Grade
Science	11	56	Adequate	Above Grade
JUDGMENTS OF TOO EASY				
Reading	4	62	Adequate	Below Grade
Reading	4	60	Inadequate	Below Grade
Reading	8	67	Adequate	Below Grade
Social studies	6	59	Adequate	Below Grade
Social studies	8	59	Adequate	Below Grade
Social studies	11	67	Adequate	On Grade
Social studies	11	67	Adequate	On Grade
Science	8	58	Adequate	On Grade

with their ability to comprehend their textbooks. These findings suggest that perhaps students should be involved more often in decisions about their textbooks and that their ideas may be a fairly reliable assessment of books that are appropriate for them.

Why did students judge the passages as they did? When asked, the most common responses were about vocabulary and concepts. For example, a fourth-grade student thought her passage was about right because she could "understand all the words and tell what they mean." When asked why she judged her passage hard, a sixth-grade student said, "The words make it hard; I can't remember them." "I would have said easy," she continued, "if it had different words." An eighth-grade student described a passage as having "hard ideas that were hard to understand," and an eleventh-grade student said his passage was hard because "the ideas were too technical." Generally, younger students seemed to talk of "words," while older students spoke of "ideas."

Aspects of organization, explanation, or depth of treatment were mentioned frequently, but mostly by students in the higher grades. A well-organized passage was judged about right by one eighth-grade student who could, in his words, "summarize it in my head." In other cases, however, these features seemed to lead students to different conclusions. For example, an eleventh-grade student said a passage was "too easy" because "it gave so much information," while an eighth-grade student rated a passage as "too hard" for the same reason.

Only about 10% of the students gave interest or enjoyment as a reason for their ratings. Such a limited number is noteworthy, since motivating students and providing interesting materials is a top priority of many teachers. Yet no students rated a passage "too hard" because it was uninteresting.

There were mixed results with regard to what students said about how difficult their books should be, and whether they would prefer them to be easier, harder, or just about the same as the passages taken from the books they used. Just as most students judged their passages to be about right, most of them also said that they preferred textbooks at about the same level of difficulty as the ones they were using. (Note, however, that except in the area of reading, most of their textbooks could be classified as difficult for them.) When preferences for easier books were expressed, these generally came from students with low cloze scores. But when books were found to be above grade level, students who scored higher on the cloze tests occasionally wanted easier books.

Students whose ideal textbook would be on the same difficulty level as the ones being used added comments such as, "It gives facts without extra details or hard words." "It explains a lot." "I can find answers to questions." "It's not boring, and I can understand it." One said simply, "I can read the words."

Many of those who wanted less difficult textbooks mentioned that they were also influenced by vocabulary and concepts, which they preferred to be easier.

Those who wanted their textbooks to be harder said that harder books enhanced their learning. For example, one student commented, "I can improve my reading by reading hard words." Another added, "If it is not hard enough to be interesting, you do not think about it long enough to learn." Still another said, "I read harder books more carefully to understand the words." Students who wanted more difficult books also seemed to be quite confident in their abilities as independent learners and added remarks such as, "I like challenge" or, "I can take anything they dish out!"

Some students' preferences were influenced by whether assistance from the teacher was available, as indicated by statements such as, "Harder passages are better for learning, but you need someone to answer questions." "The teacher helps us understand what we read by relating what happened then to what is happening now." "He uses our own words and experiences, when the book is hard." This correspondence has long been known in reading instruction and by cognitive psychologists. On the whole, these students assumed help was available from the teacher, and they tended to prefer more difficult books.

In summary, the students we interviewed seemed satisfied with the difficulty of the reading, social studies, and science textbooks they were using. Although not consistently, their judgments seemed to be influenced by the readability of their books as well as by their ability to understand them. Students with inadequate comprehension of a passage tended to rate it hard, and the passages so rated were usually above the students' tested reading achievement levels. Easy ratings were usually given by students with adequate cloze comprehension scores, and their textbooks were more often on or below their own reading levels.

Students in all grades tended to be quite satisfied with the difficulty levels of the books they were using. Those who preferred easier books were using books with readability levels above their own reading levels, and they had difficulty comprehending them. Most students said they preferred harder books when they had assistance from a teacher.

After their preferences had been stated, we asked students if they had any suggestions for improving their books. A typical fourth-grade student wrote, "Writers should use shorter, easier, more pronounceable words." In contrast was a suggestion from an eighth-grade student who felt that books could be harder or provide more depth of treatment: "Books should explain more, give more detail, provide more information." Another recommendation, made by an eleventh-grade student, was quite similar to ones suggested in some current criticisms, namely, that textbooks "didn't encourage debate" and needed to encourage students to come to their own conclusions about what they learn.

CHAPTER 9

Textbook-Selection Committees

At the present, 22 states and most large city districts — Buffalo, Hartford, Chicago, and St. Louis, for example — use adoption procedures for selection of textbooks. Usually several books are "listed," from which local school districts can make their choices. This is done on a regular cycle, every 5 or 8 years. The procedures regulating most selections of textbooks require decision making in full view of the public. The procedures followed in the large city districts tend to be similar to those followed in state adoptions.

As noted in previous chapters, public criticism of textbooks used in schools began to increase in the 1970s. These concerns included such issues as level of challenge, quality, and content, and they naturally led to inquiries as to whether adoption committees were sufficiently informed to make appropriate selections. Research by Farr and Tulley (1985) pointed to the similarity in textbook selection among states and to the lack of disciplined, systematic approaches. Few investigators found selection committees to be concerned with recommendations from the research base or with the outcomes of publishers' field tests. Indeed, the books most frequently selected tended to be those published by the largest, most reputable publishing houses (Farr, Tulley, & Powell, 1987).

Our study was concerned with how committees evaluated suitable difficulty for the students in their various grades. Toward this end, letters of inquiry were sent to 20 state adoption committees, half of which responded with information about factors related to difficulty, who evaluates textbooks, and what criteria are used.

We also requested copies of criteria and instructions used by the adoption committees for evaluating textbooks and those sent to publishers who submit books for adoption.

ATTENTION TO MATCHING

None of the adoption committees reported using a procedure for evaluating textbooks by matching their levels of difficulty to students' reading abilities. Several, however, indicated some concern with the issue. For example, one reply stated that, "because standardized testing supports the realization that the majority of our students are able to achieve at an 'above average' level, we seek materials of optimal challenge." Other references were made to grade levels and reading levels, to opportunities for making "instructional adjustments" and readability checks, to piloting texts with students of varying reading skill levels, and the like.

One committee reported seeking to "identify programs that provide opportunities for pacing instruction to meet the needs of a diverse student population," although the teacher, they said, is ultimately responsible for placement of students in readers. Another committee used two lists of criteria for basal readers, one evaluating texts for average pupils, the other for below-average students, with the latter calling for more explicit questions, greater vocabulary control, fewer new words, and more repetitions.

ASSESSMENTS OF OPTIMAL DIFFICULTY

We examined the committees' replies to see what factors were important to them in making an optimal match between students and texts, and how those factors were determined.

Evaluation checklists were used for this purpose by all committees, although the factors to be judged and ways of evaluating them varied from a three-point scale to general descriptions. The factors included in most of the checklists were readability, vocabulary, skill development, and adaptability for different skill levels. Readability was included in almost all checklists, for both content textbooks and basal readers. Assessments of readability included attention to aspects such as ease, style, challenge, sentence structure, legibility, print size, and format.

Several committees attempted to relate text difficulty to students' reading abilities, that is, whether it was geared to slow, average, or superior readers; whether the majority of their students could read it; and whether it was suited to the needs of poor readers.

Attention was also given to the readability of support materials such as workbooks, for, as one respondent wrote, "although widely used as reinforcement and as independent activities, workbooks frequently contain directions and content at a higher level than the reading books."

In summary, all committees reported giving attention to difficulty levels in selecting textbooks, but only a few specified how it was to be determined.

Another feature of textbooks assessed by most committees was vocabulary, particularly in evaluating reading textbooks. Attention was given to how new words were introduced, repeated, and maintained. Also evaluated were the difficulty or grade level of words and the vocabulary skills taught, particularly in content textbooks.

The way in which textbooks provided for skill development was also assessed by most committees. It was interesting that the sequence and pacing of skills and learning strategies were evaluated more often for basal readers than for content textbooks.

About half of the committees evaluated the adaptability of the textbooks for students on varying levels of achievement or "skills acquisition." They looked at the availability of supplementary materials to meet varying student needs and at whether the pace of lessons could be modified for more and less able readers.

Factors evaluated less frequently were content (appropriateness, accuracy, and the like), bias, and whether the textbook provided assessment procedures. It is interesting to note the considerable gap between the assessment committees and the publishers we surveyed, who considered bias and content representing different ethnic groups of greatest importance, greater than their strong concern for suitable difficulty (see Chapter 3).

STANDARDS APPLIED

Few of the committees mentioned using different standards for the different grades or different standards for students at different reading levels. In fact, although all but one committee reported using readability formulas as one procedure for evaluating textbooks, none said they used a particular readability score as a standard for a particular grade. Instead, respondents said only that they ascertained the readability of textbooks targeted for the various grades, particularly in the selection of basal readers. One respondent commented that a responsibility of the textbook-selection committee was to determine if the materials designated by the publisher for a particular grade were in fact appropriate for students working at that grade level. However, the level of difficulty considered appropriate for each grade was not indicated.

Another said that the committee considered questions such as whether the level of a text was suited to average and below-average pupils and whether there was a smooth transition in difficulty between grades. Although these concerns were shared by other committees, none specified how suitability was determined or what would be considered a smooth transition.

The evaluation forms and materials sent by the committees did not, generally, provide the standards by which evaluators could judge the appropriateness of a text for students of different reading abilities within a grade, although two respondents described the use of more than one reading series to accommodate the different reading levels within the same grade. One committee mentioned selecting multiple textbooks for intermediate-grade students, and others noted that, in the primary grades, adjustments for ability could be made by within-class grouping and additional help for below-average students.

Overall, concerns for student and textbook matching were mainly in terms of adjustments for students of average and below-average reading abilities. Few committees mentioned adjustments for above-average readers. Fewer still gave criteria or standards against which textbooks could be evaluated to insure an optimal match. Thus the procedures used by textbook committees were similar to those reported by the teachers and publishers we surveyed and interviewed. They used various measures to evaluate text difficulty and to match it to student ability, particularly to those of below-average reading ability, but they reported no standards to be used for evaluating an optimal level of challenge.

SELECTION PARTICIPANTS

To our questions regarding who participates in the adoption process, almost all the committees reported that a central administrative board, composed of supervisory personnel, principals, and curriculum specialists, coordinated the text-selection process. School administrators and teachers also participated as members of selection committees. When a central board existed apart from other evaluation bodies, it was usually responsible for developing a list of approved texts, which then underwent subsequent evaluation by another committee. At some point in the textbook review process, teachers became involved. When content-area textbooks were selected, content-area specialists and teachers usually served as evaluators, and reading specialists usually participated in evaluating basal reading series.

Students and parents also participated in some evaluations. One respondent described piloting textbooks with students and using their judgments in her evaluation. In another case students' and parents' involvement was also sought, but only when funds permitted.

SELECTION CRITERIA

All respondents said that administrative personnel were responsible for developing the evaluative criteria for textbooks. Several committees indicated that teachers and parents also participated, particularly in setting basal reader criteria; but, for most, responsibility generally rested with an administrative board.

All but one committee said they used different criteria for different subjects. Their checklists indicated that criteria used for evaluating content-area textbooks were less numerous and less specific than those used for evaluating reading textbooks.

Our question regarding what criteria were sent to the publishers who submitted textbooks for adoption was answered by only one respondent. He reported that his committee presented reading textbook publishers with a list of criteria similar to the one the committee itself used, and asked them to respond to them in both oral presentations and written reports. None of the committees reported sending evaluation criteria to publishers of content-area textbooks.

SUMMARY AND CONCLUSIONS

Responses to our inquiry into evaluating text difficulty and optimal challenge indicated a deep concern with making appropriate textbook selections, as expressed in elaborate checklists on factors that needed evaluation. But these checklists, as well as their less formal responses, revealed many difficulties and dilemmas.

For example, the major emphasis of the selection processes seemed to be on basal readers, with little attention given to the selection of content-area textbooks. We wonder why this is so, when basal reader publishers, in particular, make available considerable data on content, method, and difficulty, grade for grade, so that textbook committees can compare one publisher's books with another's. In contrast, little such information is provided by publishers of content-area textbooks, which would seem to necessitate more extensive analysis by the selection committees. For the same reason, more help is also needed in effecting optimal matching of content-area textbooks with curriculum objectives and with the instructional needs and reading abilities of students.

Nonetheless, when respondents expressed concern for selecting textbooks suitable for students of "average" and "below-average" reading abilities, it was most often with regard to basal reading textbooks, even though reading series generally include several books for a single grade and it is common for reading textbooks intended for a lower grade to be used by less able students in higher grades. By contrast, for content-area textbooks, since the content of a particular subject must be learned by all students irrespective of reading ability, and because only one book is used for each grade, the problem of an optimal match for students of varying reading abilities is greater. We wonder, therefore, why so few guidelines were given for estimating optimal student/text matching for subject-matter textbooks.

Generally, the factors noted most often on checklists were readability (ease, style, challenge), vocabulary, skill development, and adaptability for students of different reading abilities and skill levels. There seemed to be no question that the committees considered text difficulty an important issue. These are similar to the views of publishers and teachers found in our surveys and interviews (see Chapters 3 and 4).

Yet we get a sense from the selection-committee responses that things are not as clear as they may seem. There is a sense of vagueness about the criteria used for evaluating suitable difficulty. Missing, particularly, were standards for determining an optimal match. For example, although checklists for evaluating basal readers were quite extensive and detailed, standards were not given or suggested. Also, while all committees used readability measures as criteria, none specified the readability levels that were considered appropriate for pupils of given reading abilities. The impression we get is that it is sufficient to do a readability analysis, regardless of scores obtained. This would be similar to saying that taking children's temperatures is sufficient for establishing their health, whether there is a fever or not.

This came as somewhat of a surprise to us, since, in the current discontent with textbooks, many have blamed the poor quality of their writing on the pressures put upon publishers by the textbook-adoption committees for specific readability scores. It was therefore surprising that none of the checklists sent to us included readability scores for the different texts for the different grades.

It was also interesting that the adoption committees did not suggest standards of optimal difficulty, even in broad terms. This lack of specificity was found as well in the views of teachers and publishers (see Chapters 3 and 4) and in the teacher's manuals and methods textbooks for reading, social studies, and science (see Chapter 6). Also similar to our previous findings was the textbook-adoption committees' greater concern for the average and below-average than for the above-average reader. Indeed, most statements regarding text difficulty addressed only the needs of the former.

While the responses from the committees yielded interesting and relevant knowledge, also intriguing was information that was not forthcoming. Although we encouraged respondents to comment freely, none commented about their satisfaction or dissatisfaction with the textbooks currently in use, or on whether those available met the needs of their school system or their students. There was also no comment regarding the levels of difficulty assigned to textbooks by publishers; rather, there seemed to be a general acceptance of them. Although some mention was made about the need for harder textbooks, there was little indication that this should be given priority.

Also noteworthy were the great numbers and variety of factors included on most checklists. We wonder whether, with this abundance, it is possible for committee members to establish priorities or to focus on the relationships among factors. We found no clear suggestions as to how such a synthesis was to be accomplished or how it would lead to final decisions in adoptions.

Our inquiry of textbook-adoption committees, as well as our surveys of publishers and educators, gives further evidence that they seem to use the same criteria for evaluating textbooks. It would be of interest to know why. Is it because they all use the same knowledge base from the available research? This may be so, but it is significant that none of them referred specifically to research, in any of our surveys. Or is it because they exist in a kind of symbiotic relationship to each other? In such a system, it would be difficult for publishers to be competitive and successful if they did not pay attention to the trends in the criteria to be used in adoptions and in the preferences of teachers and textbook-adoption committees. In turn, the teachers and committees would be sent informative and persuasive brochures and invited to attend educational conferences sponsored by publishers, designed to present their textbooks as meeting the needs of students and teachers. Essentially, if schools differed significantly from the major publishing houses, they would not have books to buy; and if publishers differed significantly from the criteria used by textbook committees, they could not sell the books they produced.

If criteria were to be changed by only the publishers, or the teachers, or the adoption committees, some difficulties would arise. This is just what happened recently, when California rejected all science textbooks. The publishers who sought adoption in that state modified their books to comply with California's new criteria. Should harder textbooks be required and adopted by some textbook-adoption committees, changes might occur in the production of such books by some publishers. If these were bought by schools, chances are that the other publishers would follow with harder books.

In reality, even the most comprehensive checklists and criteria for selection need to be updated regularly. If they are to serve as standards for selecting the best materials, they have to be changed as students' abilities change and as knowledge about optimal difficulty is refined through educational research. However, the selection process seems to be essentially conservative with regard to new research findings. Thus, even if the educational research indicates the need for a change in criteria, publishers may resist implementing the change for fear that adoption committees may not have incorporated the new research findings into their selection procedures and that teachers would not be ready to accept them.

Educational research findings seem to have helped alert both publishers and textbook-selection committees to textbook factors that will improve learning. The guidelines developed from these research findings, however, have not been sufficiently specific or practical. The research has suggested a direction rather than a standard. For example, from about 1920 to 1970, educational research stressed the need for easy textbooks. The research of the 1970s suggested that the books had perhaps become too easy. By the 1980s, there was a critical outburst decrying the lack of rigor. To avoid such swings, we need ongoing research on standards of optimal difficulty for different students, for different content areas, and for different instructional tasks. This kind of research would be of great help to selection committees as well as to publishers and teachers.

CHAPTER 10

Conclusions and Recommendations

We have come a long way in our study of textbooks. The summaries found in the preceding chapters present the findings from our various analyses—the research review, the opinions of publishers and teachers, classroom uses of textbooks, students' views of their textbooks, and others. We present, here, our broader questions, conclusions, and recommendations.

HOW IMPORTANT
IS SUITABLE READING LEVEL?

In the opinions of the publishers, teachers, students, and textbook-adoption committees we surveyed, suitable reading level is of great importance in students' learning from texts. These views are in line with the accumulated research findings on text difficulty of the past 70 years. In fact, the publishers who responded to our surveys reported that they thought suitable reading level was more important than most other aspects of textbook publishing. Only a book's content and treatment of controversial and sensitive issues were considered more important.

Our tests of students' understanding of their texts also indicated that the text's difficulty was significantly related to what they learned from the text. Further, students' judgments of their ability to read their texts, and their tested comprehension of it, corresponded very well with the difficulty of the various passages they attempted.

Why, then, in light of this strong and continuous evidence on the importance of suitable difficulty, has there been recent opposition to the concept? Why is there a growing tendency to say that literary quality and student interest should be the criteria for book selection? One explanation may be the misuse of tools to measure difficulty by some writers and editors. Readability formulas have been used to rewrite texts to grade-level specifications, a practice that has been discouraged by readability researchers since the early 1920s. To apply formulas in this way is incorrect and it may have produced texts that lacked organization and cohesion. It is imperative that users of formulas understand that they were developed to serve as measures of difficulty, not as guides for writing. Yet it is questionable whether one can blame the existence of incoherent writing in textbooks on quantitative measures of difficulty. One can certainly find examples of incoherent writing that predates the existence and use of readability measures.

If quantitative measures of difficulty are used incorrectly by educational writers and editors, then one solution is to train writers and editors in their proper uses. To throw out the concept because it has been misused by some may make it more difficult to effect an optimal match of students and textbooks. Indeed, a recent NAEP *Reading Report Card* confirms the primary importance of text difficulty on reading comprehension, noting that "three factors [affect] students' reading proficiency: the complexity of the material they were asked to read, their familiarity with the subject matter, and the kinds of questions asked" (Mullis & Jenkins, 1990, p. 22).

Our examination of the teacher's manuals accompanying the textbooks of the late 1980s also reveals decreased concern for text difficulty. The manuals of the late 1970s and early 1980s suggested the use of readability formulas for estimating text difficulty, but most of the more recent manuals do not. Instead they talk of difficulty in terms of the style of the text or of its being teachable or learnable. Since the readability levels of the late 1980s texts were essentially the same as those published in the early 1980s, it would appear that publishers have continued to use readability measurement for estimating difficulty, although they discuss its use differently.

It has also become popular to say that textbooks are suitable if they are interesting and contain high-quality writing, and that it matters little how difficult they are. While quality of writing and interesting content have always been considered important in the development and selection of textbooks, it should be noted that we know little about their influence on learning from text. They have been and still remain difficult to assess with any degree of objectivity. Suitable difficulty, on the other hand, is a potent factor in learning from text and it is relatively easy to measure objectively.

ARE THE TEXTBOOKS TOO EASY? OR TOO HARD?

Whether the textbooks students are using are too easy or too hard depends on the content of the textbooks, the grade for which they were developed, and the reading abilities of the students using them.

Overall, our study found that the reading textbooks used by most students were the easiest — less difficult than the social studies and science textbooks, grade for grade. This was so because of the policy of grouping students by reading ability for reading instruction and using a reading textbook to match the reading ability of the group. Another policy, that of using below-grade-level reading textbooks for below-average readers but not above-grade-level textbooks for above-average readers, further contributed to the overall easy rating received by these books.

Yet we found that the reading textbooks, which presented the least challenge to the students, received the greatest amount of instructional time and emphasis. The harder social studies and science textbooks used in the elementary grades received about half the instructional time devoted to the reading textbooks.

The social studies and science books were harder overall; furthermore, the lower the grade, the harder they were in comparison to students' reading abilities. Most of the science and social studies textbooks for the fourth grade were above the reading levels of the majority of the children using them. They were also above the reading ability of the fourth-grade norming population on the Metropolitan Achievement Test.

The sixth- and eighth-grade science and social studies textbooks were more closely matched to the reading abilities of those who used them. The eleventh-grade books, on the other hand, were below the reading level of most of the students who used them.

The science textbooks tended, overall, to be harder than the social studies books. This stems from the use of a high load of specialized and technical vocabularies in the science textbooks. The social studies textbooks tended to express difficult concepts in familiar words, thus having lower estimates of difficulty. When differences in the disciplines are taken into account, the difficulty of the science and social studies books may be more similar than different.

In the final analysis, perhaps the best explanation for the relative difficulty of fourth-grade science and social studies texts is the change in content and in reading tasks in the fourth grade. In the first three grades, the reading matter is usually familiar. At about the fourth grade, when reading becomes a tool for learning, the textbooks contain more worldly knowledge and more abstract, literary, and technical words and ideas. These make a textbook difficult to read. One may ask whether it is essential for the social studies and science books to be so difficult at the fourth grade. Is it necessary to teach so much at the very beginning of the systematic study of science and social studies? Can educators and publishers agree on what is essential for fourth-grade social studies and science and what can wait until later grades?

We need to look at fourth-grade texts for still another reason: This is the grade when the reading achievement of lower-income children has been found to begin to decelerate (Chall, Jacobs, & Baldwin, 1990). This seems to stem mainly from a lack of familiarity with abstract literary and technical words — words used increasingly in the content-area textbooks in the intermediate and upper elementary grades. Through grade three, when the reading matter tends to be more familiar and unspecialized, the reading scores of low-income and mainstream children are similar. Since deceleration seems to come at about fourth grade, it is particularly important that the difficulty of textbooks in the fourth grade make the transition as smooth as possible for all children and especially for those whose reading scores have a tendency to decelerate at this point.

Another grade that needs attention is the eleventh. Most of the social studies textbooks for the eleventh grade published in the early 1980s were below the reading levels of the students in that grade. Those published between 1987 and 1989 seemed to be even easier. It may well be that the growing ease of the eleventh-grade texts is the publishers' response to the low reading achievement of 17-year-olds found on several national reading assessments (see Applebee, Langer, & Mullis, 1989). Yet, if challenging textbooks contribute positively to students' development, it would seem that lowering the difficulty still further may have an effect opposite from the one desired. Are the schools and publishers taking the easier way out for the eleventh-grade textbooks? Are they putting too much emphasis on the immediate learning of content and too little on developing the higher levels of reading needed for a postsecondary education and for life in a high-technology, high-information age?

It would seem that over and above the need to monitor textbook difficulty for the various grades and students within grades, we need to study them for their long-term effects on reading and language development. (See Chall et al., 1977, in this connection.)

HOW HAVE TEXTBOOKS CHANGED?

We were able to compare the difficulty of eleventh-grade history textbooks over a period of more than three decades. This was possible because readability data on eleventh-grade history texts published during the 1960s was available from our earlier study (Chall et al., 1977) and could be compared with the two analyses reported in the present study — books published between 1974 and 1982, and those published between 1985 and 1989. Overall, the readability levels of all three groups of eleventh-grade history textbooks published over this thirty-year period was about the same — grade level in each group averaged 9–10. The books became larger, however, going from about 700 pages typical for the 1960–1970 books, to 800 for the late 1970s books, to around 1,000 for the late 1980s books.

Unfortunately, such a thirty-year comparison was not possible for the fourth- and eighth-grade science, social studies, and reading textbooks because the grades and subjects analyzed in the earlier study were not comparable to the two reported here. (See Chapter 5 for changes in textbooks published over the last 15 years).

DO TEXTBOOKS PROVIDE A GOOD MATCH?

Most students could comprehend adequately texts that were on their reading level and below, as well as those that were one to two grades above their tested reading ability. This was true for students who could read on grade level and above. Those who read at about two or more grade levels below the norms did not do well on materials a grade or two above their reading levels. This group constituted about one-fourth of the student population. They were in regular classrooms, exposed to the regular curriculum. They were not in special education classes for the handicapped. Such students found the assigned social studies and science textbooks too difficult. Only their reading textbooks could be read with ample understanding.

The usual suggestions made in content-area methods textbooks for resolving the inadequate match between less able readers and their content-area textbooks are that teachers use easier books on the same topic for the below-average readers. But our analysis of textbooks indicates that such books do not seem to exist. Other suggestions are that teachers rewrite on a lower reading level portions of the required text. This strikes us as unrealistic. It is extremely difficult to simplify text while at the same time keeping the content similar and accurate. It is also very time-consuming. Indeed, professional educational writers and editors are increasingly being criticized for doing it poorly.

One way that many teachers solve the problem is by not using any textbooks at all with students who read poorly. Instead, they lecture, use pictures to demonstrate, or direct discussions. This also appears to us to be a less-than-satisfactory solution. While the poor readers may learn some content this way, they cannot develop their reading abilities if they do not read.

This is an area we believe to be of greatest need in educational publishing. There is a need for textbooks and instructional materials that can be used by students in the lowest quartile in reading — those reading two or more grades below the norms. Such materials are needed for learning content and for developing reading and language proficiencies.

The students who read poorly were remarkably sensitive to their needs. Most wanted books that they could read and understand. They knew why they could not understand their textbooks. The younger ones (fourth and sixth graders) said it was the hard words that made their texts difficult. The older students (eighth and eleventh graders) said they had difficulty because of their book's organization and ideas.

Another group not adequately served was those who read about two grades or more above the norms. Their reading textbooks, especially, provided little or no challenge, since they were matched to students' grade placement, not their reading levels. Many students were aware of this and said, in their interviews, that they preferred harder books because they learned more new words and ideas from them. Since harder reading textbooks were readily available, one may ask why they were not used with the more able readers, as were the easier reading textbooks for the less able readers. This practice of using grade-level reading textbooks for those who read two or more grades above the norms has changed little through the years, although it has been repeatedly questioned (see Chall, 1967, 1983). It would appear that, for various administrative reasons, most teachers do not use a reading textbook that is above the student's grade placement. The reason most often mentioned is really a question: If the third-grade teacher uses fourth-grade books, what is the fourth-grade teacher to do?

In sum, the subject-matter textbooks published in the United States represented a rather narrow range of difficulty for each grade we analyzed, more narrow than the range of reading ability found among students. It was also narrower than the range found on standardized tests. Although the publishers described their textbooks as being developed for "wide use" or for "more able" or "less able" readers, our analysis found them suitable mainly for the middle range of achievement within each grade. Practically none of the content textbooks seemed to be written for the students in the lowest quartile in reading. Further, the books that publishers labeled for less able readers were often more difficult than those labeled for a wide audience or for more able readers.

Only the types of questions asked in the textbooks, workbooks, and teacher's manuals seemed to differ: The books for the below-average readers had more factual and fewer inferential questions than the ones for the average and above-average readers.

On the whole, the average readers for each grade were served best, the above-average less well, and the lowest quarter in reading ability were served least by the available textbooks.

IS OPTIMAL CHALLENGE IMPORTANT FOR ALL READERS?

Teachers as well as publishers seemed to be more concerned with challenging the better than the poorer readers. Few said that the poorer readers needed to be challenged by their textbooks, and yet we know, from both research and theory, that they, too, benefit from challenge. One hypothesis for why this gap exists is that both teachers and publishers have internalized an assumption that has dominated textbook development and selection for many decades, namely, that the easier the book, the better, particularly for below-average readers. Indeed, most of the methods textbooks and the teacher's manuals we analyzed cautioned against using textbooks that might be too hard and that might frustrate the less able reader. It is interesting that none offered the parallel caution that texts not be too easy.

The cloze-test comprehension scores of our below-average readers indicated that they could, like those of average and above-average reading ability, read and comprehend texts that were about a year above their own reading levels. We also found from our interviews that most students preferred a challenge, particularly when the teacher provided instruction and guidance. We recommend, therefore, that teachers and publishers reexamine their views on an optimal match for all readers and particularly for above- and below-average readers. The same principles are appropriate for all students. When instruction is guided by a teacher or knowledgeable peer, books that are at or somewhat above the student's level of reading achievement will generally enhance reading development (see Vygotsky, 1978).

Teachers need more knowledge about how to estimate text difficulty and how to effect an optimal match with students' reading abilities. Such information should be included in their teacher education, in their methods textbooks, and in the teacher's manuals accompanying students' textbooks.

WHAT IS THE OPTIMAL LENGTH OF TEXT AND NUMBER OF ILLUSTRATIONS?

The textbooks have become larger and heavier, and the number of illustrations has grown; all textbook watchers agree on this point. At each grade we studied — fourth, sixth, eighth, and eleventh — the social studies and science textbooks had one or more illustrations per page of text.

No one seems to know if the bigger books with their numerous illustrations help the student learn better, or motivate the student more. But everyone seems to be caught in the dilemma of increasing text size and number of illustrations. Publishers seem to fear that, if they cut down on text size and number of illustrations, they will lose a competitive edge in adoptions and sales. No one seems to know if teachers and students really want bigger books and more pictures, either. None of the students we interviewed mentioned illustrations when they talked of their preferences. Yet this does not prevent publishers from including 1,000 illustrations in 1,000 pages of text in an eleventh-grade social studies textbook. The size and weight make the textbooks increasingly difficult to lift and carry. We wonder how students manage when they have homework that requires the use of two or three of these textbooks. We need research on optimal book size, including optimal number of illustrations.

DO TEXTBOOKS TEACH STUDY SKILLS ALONG WITH CONTENT?

The teacher's manuals for the social studies and science textbooks contained a considerable number of suggestions for teaching vocabulary, comprehension, and study skills, but these could best be described as general advice, rather than as specific guidance. Thus, although most of the books gave teachers general suggestions on teaching vocabulary, few suggested which words in the textbook needed special attention. Nor did they give specific suggestions for how to teach the difficult words in the book. Also, no advice was given on how to test whether the students learned the new vocabulary.

More direct aid was given teachers on improving students' comprehension of the text, with some textbooks providing the actual questions. On the whole, the textbooks for the earlier grades contained more factual questions, while the texts for the higher grades contained more inferential questions. The science texts asked fewer inferential questions than the social studies, grade for grade, as would be expected by the differences in the disciplines.

The textbooks targeted by the publishers to the below-average readers also tended to have more factual and fewer inferential questions. Since some below-average readers have difficulty making inferences, it is puzzling why teachers were not advised as to how to help them. It would seem as if the writers and editors were concerned more with the "immediate success" of the less able readers than with their long-term reading and language development. Much more attention needs to be paid to the teaching of higher-level reading and thinking skills to less able readers.

SHOULD QUANTITATIVE MEASUREMENT CONTINUE?

Our study confirmed the research of the past 70 years on the essential validity of quantitative measures of reading ability and text difficulty. The standardized reading scores of the pupils we tested predicted how well they would comprehend reading selections of different levels of difficulty. Also, the readability scores predicted students' ability to comprehend the cloze passages; that is, the harder the readability level of a passage, the higher the reading scores needed to understand it.

We also found considerable similarity between quantitative and qualitative measures of text difficulty. For example, students' cloze-test comprehension scores, their judgments of passage difficulty (whether easy, just right, or hard), and the readability scores of the passages were all positively associated. Also, the qualitative estimates of reading stages and question difficulty were positively correlated with the quantitative readability scores.

We therefore recommend that quantitative measures of student ability as well as of text difficulty not be abandoned in favor of qualitative ones, as some recommend. The purpose of the assessment may indicate the use of one or the other, but, if a qualitative assessment is preferred, it will generally give similar results when compared to the quantitative assessment. Whether qualitative assessment is superior to quantitative assessment is not revealed by this study, although findings from the application of a reading-stage model did provide complementary insight for our quantitative analysis. Additional research could certainly be helpful here.

WHAT ACCOUNTS FOR THE CONSENSUS ON TEXTBOOKS?

Educational publishers, teachers, and textbook adoption committees seem to hold similar views on textbooks. The differences between publishers' and teachers' opinions on difficulty were slight; one set of views could be substituted for the other. Why would this be? Should one not expect an adversarial stance between them, with publishers as the producers of the books and the teachers as the consumers?

The recent action of the State of California — refusing to adopt any of the math and science textbooks offered it by the publishers — is rare. It seemed to be settled rather quickly, however, when the publishers modified their books to meet the requests of California.

This suggests not an adversarial role between textbook developers and users of texts, but one of cooperation and consensus. Indeed, if the publishers had refused to accommodate California's requests, the students would have been without new textbooks, and the state would not have complied with the legal requirement that new textbooks be purchased after a given number of years.

Educational publishers, as well as schools, tend to accommodate to a climate of opinion. Thus, when the early research led to a consensus that the easier the book, the better, educational publishers produced easier books. Moreover, they continued to do so even after the research evidence ceased to support it, evidently because teachers and administrators still held to that belief.

In short, textbooks result from a kind of consensus among publishers, teachers, adoption committees, and researchers. The tendency to "agree" comes also from the fact that there is a great deal of overlap in the roles played by many in educational publishing. Thus, the leading scholars and researchers are the authors, editors, and consultants for the leading educational publishers; and most editors and sales and management people in educational publishing are former teachers. This overlap of roles is particularly visible in the production of reading textbooks. For more than half a century, the authors and consultants of the most widely used basal reading programs have been the leading university professors and reading researchers, the authors of methods textbooks for prospective teachers, and officers of the leading reading and language arts associations.

CAN WE IMPROVE TEXTBOOK-ADOPTION PROCEDURES?

During the past decade, many proposals for improving the quality of textbooks have focused on the need to improve the process of selecting and adopting textbooks. While such reforms are important, our study suggests that they may not be as effective as hoped for and may ultimately lead to disappointment. Textbook-adoption committees, we learned from our survey, are grappling with the same questions and using the same criteria as are publishers and teachers. The criteria they rely on for selection are therefore as strong and as weak as those used by teachers and publishers. Indeed, a recent study that compared the basal reader selections of adoption and nonadoption states found no real differences in the textbooks selected. Both selected the most widely known and widely used programs, produced by the largest and oldest publishing houses (Farr, Tulley, & Rayford, 1987).

Many textbook adoption committees use check lists to assess content, level of difficulty, and other aspects of textbook appropriateness and quality. However, these do not seem to include standards against which to assess these factors. Further, it is not clear which of these factors should receive priority. Thus, while space was provided for checking off illustrations, there was no way of assessing how many illustrations are optimal or what kinds of illustrations help students to understand their text better and find it more interesting.

Textbook-adoption procedures will be improved as our knowledge of text characteristics in relation to students' abilities improves and also as we learn more about what is learned from textbooks.

HOW CAN RESEARCH AND ITS USES BE EXTENDED?

For an area of education as important as textbooks, there is, surprisingly, a very limited commitment to research. On certain issues, such as text difficulty and its measurement, there is considerable knowledge that has been validated over a period of about 70 years. But this research, and particularly the applied aspects of it, needs regular updating. Thus, while the early conclusions in the 1920s and 1930s that the textbooks were too difficult may have been correct for their time, they were not correct for all times. What was not done, and what needed to be done, was to monitor and test regularly whether the changes in the textbooks were optimal for student learning.

We also need to study many other questions, for example, what the best size is for textbooks and what is a helpful number of illustrations. We need to know the kinds of instructional materials that are most useful for students who are in the bottom quarter in reading ability — and how to produce such materials. Most of all, we need a more positive attitude toward research and its uses. It has been reported that school systems seldom ask for the research evidence on the effectiveness of given published programs. Also, although field-testing data are available, few schools ask for it (Squire, 1988). This seems also to be characteristic of some textbook critics. They seldom cite research evidence on the issues they discuss and tend instead to base their recommendations on their own impressions.

Most of the current writing on textbooks seems to be oblivious to past practices as well as past research. While this weakness is also widespread in other areas of education (see Slavin, 1989), it has become particularly evident in the recent literature on textbooks, where most writers have paid little attention to the existing research on the issues they are discussing and have failed to suggest the need for research where views are conflicting.

WHO IS RESPONSIBLE?

It would be futile to continue playing the blaming game of the past decade—blaming, in turn, the publishers, the teachers, the textbook-adoption committees, and the assessment instruments for the quality of our textbooks. In truth, all are responsible, each in a particular way. But these responsibilities seem to be changing. For example, some publishers now play the role of both publisher and author by producing "in-house" programs under the publisher's name. Can one criticize such tools the same way one criticizes the books of an independent author? If so, can't the publishers turn the criticism around by claiming that the books were created to comply with the wishes of the teachers? But if publishers decide to take this line of defense—and after all, publishers have been known to say, "If books are not good, we must look to the teachers"—why do they do so much promoting of the uniqueness, the rightness, the research-based aspects of their texts and give such extensive support to professional conferences?

Educational publishers are alert to changing teacher interests; thus the textbook manuals that claimed in the 1970s to use "discovery learning" now say they use "cooperative learning." "Emergent literacy" has replaced "reading readiness," and a "whole language approach" is claimed by many basal reader publishers for their series published in the late 1980s. Whether or not the use of these "newer" terms has produced substantive changes in the textbooks is yet to be determined, as is whether such changes would produce better reading among the children using them.

Claiming, as some publishers do, that the ultimate responsibility for the quality of the textbooks lies with the consumers—the schools, teachers, administrators, and students—needs much discussion. After all, textbooks are not ordinary consumer products. They are used by almost all of our children. They can enhance learning or they can limit it. They have short- and long-term effects. Shouldn't publishers' products be judged by objective criteria similar to those applied to food and drugs? Or might they be required to include "truth" and "warning" labels?

Textbook authors, and publishers in the role of author, need to keep up with the best available research evidence. The publishers should field-test their programs. This does not seem to be a difficult task, since the authors and consultants of the larger publishing houses are among the nation's leading researchers. Yet it is not uncommon for these noted researchers to claim that the publishers do not listen to them!

Publishers must also be concerned that all children have quality textbooks. If books are published mainly for the largest audience—those in the middle range of reading ability—then how will we meet the needs for quality materials for those below and those above? If publishers find it unprofitable to do so, can the federal government share the responsibility, as it does for other special needs?

Another important role that educational publishers can play is in supporting basic and applied research. Most support to date has come from universities, private foundations, and the federal government, yet it has been used by publishers. For their part, they tend to support only their own field testing, but their results remain confidential and for their own use only. To its credit, the American Association of Publishers has shown a growing interest in supporting research on textbooks by awarding dissertation grants and by supporting annual conferences on textbooks. We urge that educational publishers take even greater responsibility for the support of both basic and applied research, in order to make their textbooks effective for all students and teachers.

Publishers also need to do a better job of educating their writers and editors with regard to the relevant research and tools for assessing text effectiveness. The college professors who work with educational publishers as authors or consultants also have responsibility in this area. While they are invited to join a publishing house on the basis of their strengths in scholarship and research, many seem too willing to go along with the consensus sought by the publisher. Granted, it is not pleasant to be a whistle-blower, but the scholar must be responsible for bringing the evidence from research to bear on the practical issues of text development. One can appreciate the constraints on both the publishers and the scholars, for it is a great responsibility to make decisions on, for example, a reading series that is a $25 million investment.

One wonders, also, about the possible effects of the recent consolidations of educational publishers. With fewer and bigger educational publishing houses producing the reading and subject-area textbooks for our elementary and secondary school students, will the choices available be wider or narrower? Will the overall range of difficulty of textbooks for the same grades and subjects be smaller or greater? Or will there be a tendency, even more than we found in the present study, for most textbooks to be targeted to average readers, which constitute the largest numbers? Will the consolidated publishers, instead, see the lowest and highest achievers as a "new" potential group needing their attention? Or will the existence of fewer and larger publishers of textbooks encourage the rise of smaller, more flexible educational publishers who will focus mainly on students not currently served?

We offer one other suggestion for improving the quality of textbooks— a return to the importance of the single or major author. When one person, usually a scholar in the field, has primary authorship, she or he can take responsibility for using the best available research evidence and the best known ideas from practice. If the product is good, the author can have pride in the accomplishment; if it is not, the author can take the consequences, as all authors do. The books might then be reviewed and treated as books, not as commercial products. We question, however, some recent criticisms of textbooks that call for a kind of independence and literary quality associated with trade books. While trade books may be written to the author's own specifications, one wonders whether this can or should be done for textbooks, which need to comply with curriculum and readability requirements.

Teachers, administrators, and textbook-adoption committees also have a responsibility to see that the children have quality textbooks. They make decisions as to which books are to be bought and used. If they are dissatisfied, they should let the publishers know. One thing that emerges clearly from the relevant research covering over a half-century and from this study is the symbiotic relationship among the many groups involved with textbooks. These materials are too important to be left to the decisions of any one group. As all our recommendations indicate, collaboration is necessary if improvement is to be made.

Textbooks play a significant role in the education of elementary and high school students. There is considerable evidence that textbooks have both immediate and long-term effects on learning. It has become fashionable to say that textbooks are dull and that schools should use "real" books instead. Yet the greatest writers and thinkers of the past have written with warmth of the textbooks of their childhood. Perhaps, then, it is not that textbooks are intrinsically dull, but that we have lost the art of making and using them.

APPENDIXES

REFERENCES

INDEX

ABOUT THE AUTHORS

APPENDIX A

Publisher and Teacher Survey Instruments

APPENDIX A–1
Educational Publishing Firms Participating in the Survey Studies

Addison-Wesley Publishing Company
Allyn & Bacon
American Book Company
Cambridge Book Company
The Economy Company
Educators Publishing Service
Fearon Publishers; Pitman
The Fideler Company
Follett Publishing Company
Garrard Publishing Company
Ginn and Company[1]
Globe Book Company
Harcourt Brace Jovanovich[2]
Harper & Row Publishers
D. C. Heath and Company[1]
Holt, Rinehart and Winston
Houghton Mifflin Company[1]

Laidlaw Brothers
Macmillan[1]
McDougal, Littell & Company
McGraw-Hill Book Company
McGraw-Hill/Webster Division[2]
Modern Curriculum Press
National Textbook Company
Newbury House Publishers
Open Court Publishing Company
Prentice-Hall
Random House
William H. Sadlier
Scholastic Book Services
Science Research Associates
Scott, Foresman & Company[1]
Silver Burdett Company
Steck-Vaughn Company

---

[1]Represented in both elementary and secondary samples.
[2]Secondary-level sample.

APPENDIX A-2
Survey of Secondary Textbook Publishers

1. In general, how important do Junior High and High School Teachers view a SUITABLE READING LEVEL—one that is "matched" to the reading abilities and interests of their students—compared to other considerations in textbook selection listed below? (Please check the *one* choice which is closest to your view for *each* item.)

A SUITABLE READING LEVEL IS

Much More Important	More Important	Less Important	Much Less Important	THAN:
——	——	——	——	a. adequate provision of follow-up activities.
——	——	——	——	b. adequate support materials (ditto masters, audio-visual aids, etc.).
——	——	——	——	c. appropriate concepts and ideas.
——	——	——	——	d. appropriate content.
——	——	——	——	e. availability of program-related tests.
——	——	——	——	f. clearly stated learning outcomes.
——	——	——	——	g. cost factors.
——	——	——	——	h. durability.
——	——	——	——	i. evidence of classroom pre-testing.
——	——	——	——	j. fair treatment of race, sex, ethnic groups.
——	——	——	——	k. good organization.
——	——	——	——	l. good teacher's manual.
——	——	——	——	m. recent copyright date.
——	——	——	——	n. relevant illustrations.
——	——	——	——	o. similarity of book objectives and those of subject curriculum.
——	——	——	——	p. suitable book size and format.
——	——	——	——	q. suitable type and print size.

COMMENTS ON THE IMPORTANCE OF SUITABLE READING LEVELS?

_____

_____

_____

2. In your estimate, how important is a SUITABLE READING LEVEL in Junior High and High School textbooks in comparison to the following publishing concerns? (Please check *one* choice for *each* item.)

SUITABLE READING LEVEL IS

Much More Important	More Important	Less Important	Much Less Important	THAN:
——	——	——	——	a. choice of content.

				b. choices of illustrations, charts, maps, graphs.
——	——	——	——	c. layout and typography design.
——	——	——	——	d. organization of chapters, sections, etc.
——	——	——	——	e. publication costs.
——	——	——	——	f. publication time schedule.
——	——	——	——	g. quality of writing.
——	——	——	——	h. selection of authors.
——	——	——	——	i. selection of editors.
——	——	——	——	j. treatment of race, sex, ethnic groups.
——	——	——	——	k. treatment of sensitive topics, e.g., creation, reproduction.
——	——	——	——	i. usability of teacher manual or guide.

COMMENTS ON YOUR VIEW OF SUITABLE READING LEVELS?

_____

_____

_____

3. How often are the following techniques or aids used to help make decisions regarding reading levels in Junior High and High School textbooks published by your firm?

TO HELP MAKE DECISIONS REGARDING READING LEVELS IN OUR TEXTBOOKS, WE	Always	Often	Seldom	Never
a. apply readability formulas	——	——	——	——
b. examine and count unfamiliar words	——	——	——	——
c. examine the number and difficulty of concepts and ideas	——	——	——	——
d. rely on judgments and recommendations from authors and editors	——	——	——	——
e. rely on judgments and recommendations from consultants and specialists	——	——	——	——
f. rely on judgments and recommendations from marketing personnel	——	——	——	——
g. rely on judgments and recommendations from school personnel	——	——	——	——
h. Others? Please specify _____	——	——	——	——

4. Does your firm generally try out Junior High and High School textbooks with a student population prior to publication?

        a. Yes   b. No

If you answered YES, would you indicate if the following testing methods are used in try-outs and their frequency of use?

TO TRY OUT TEXTBOOKS, WE USE	Always	Often	Seldom	Never
a. cloze tests	——	——	——	——
b. multiple-choice tests	——	——	——	——
c. oral reading tests	——	——	——	——

d. Others? Please specify _____   ____   ____   ____   ____

COMMENTS ON TECHNIQUES OR TESTING METHODS USED FOR DETERMINING SUITABLE
READING LEVEL?

_____
_____
_____

5. Often, the numbers and reading achievement of Junior High and High School students
   in instructional groups vary. Please select a *single choice* that best describes a "match"
   you would recommend to teachers as most suitable between the reading level of a textbook and the reading achievement of students in the following groups.

   a. WITH A GROUP OF 2 TO 9 STUDENTS, I would recommend the textbook read-
      ing level be matched to the reading level of: (Check one)

      ____ higher achieving students.
      ____ middle achieving students.
      ____ lower achieving students.

   b. WITH A GROUP OF 10 TO 19 STUDENTS, I would recommend the textbook
      reading level be matched to the reading level of: (Check one)

      ____ higher achieving students.
      ____ middle achieving students.
      ____ lower achieving students.

   c. WITH A GROUP OF 20 OR MORE STUDENTS, I would recommend the text-
      book reading level be matched to the reading level of: (Check one)

      ____ higher achieving students.
      ____ middle achieving students.
      ____ lower achieving students.

6. Suppose a teacher asks your advice in selecting a particular textbook for an individual
   student whose reading achievement level is known. Please select a *single choice* from
   the five on the right below that best describes a "match" you would recommend as
   most suitable between students with high, middle, and low achievement levels and a
   textbook reading level.

STUDENT ACHIEVEMENT LEVELS	TEXTBOOK READING LEVELS				
	Much Higher	Somewhat Higher	The Same	Somewhat Lower	Much Lower
a. High	____	____	____	____	____
b. Middle	____	____	____	____	____
c. Low	____	____	____	____	____

COMMENTS ON TEXTBOOK SELECTION FOR GROUPS AND INDIVIDUAL STUDENTS?

_____
_____
_____

7. In what content area is your major editorial responsibility?

   Science

   Social Studies

THANK YOU FOR YOUR ASSISTANCE!!!

(A similar form was sent to elementary textbook publishers.)

APPENDIX A–3
Survey of Junior High and High School Teachers

1. In general, when you select a textbook for instructing your classes, how important is a SUITABLE READING LEVEL—one that is "matched" to the reading abilities and interests of the students—compared to other considerations in textbook choice listed below? (Please check the *one* choice which is closest to your view for *each* item.)

A SUITABLE READING LEVEL IS

Much More Important	More Important	Less Important	Much Less Important	THAN:
_____	_____	_____	_____	a. adequate provision of follow-up activities.
_____	_____	_____	_____	b. adequate support materials (ditto masters, audio-visual aids, etc.).
_____	_____	_____	_____	c. appropriate concepts and ideas.
_____	_____	_____	_____	d. appropriate content.
_____	_____	_____	_____	e. availability of program-related tests.
_____	_____	_____	_____	f. clearly stated learning outcomes.
_____	_____	_____	_____	g. cost factors.
_____	_____	_____	_____	h. durability.
_____	_____	_____	_____	i. evidence of classroom pre-testing.
_____	_____	_____	_____	j. fair treatment of race, sex, ethnic groups.
_____	_____	_____	_____	k. good organization.
_____	_____	_____	_____	l. good teacher's manual.
_____	_____	_____	_____	m. recent copyright date.
_____	_____	_____	_____	n. relevant illustrations.
_____	_____	_____	_____	o. similarity of book objectives and those of subject curriculum.
_____	_____	_____	_____	p. suitable book size and format.
_____	_____	_____	_____	q. suitable type and print size.

COMMENTS ON THE IMPORTANCE OF SUITABLE READING LEVELS?

_____

_____

_____

2. How frequently do you use the following techniques or aids to help you decide that a textbook's reading level is suitable for your students' instruction? (Please make *one* choice for *each* technique.)

TO SELECT AN APPROPRIATE
READING LEVEL, I

	Always	Often	Seldom	Never
a. apply a readability formula	_____	_____	_____	_____
b. discuss the book with students	_____	_____	_____	_____
c. examine and count unfamiliar words	_____	_____	_____	_____

    d. examine the number and difficulty of
       concepts and ideas   ____   ____   ____   ____

    e. informally try out books with students   ____   ____   ____   ____

    f. rely on colleagues' recommendations   ____   ____   ____   ____

    g. rely on supervisor's or principal's
       recommendations   ____   ____   ____   ____

    h. use publisher's readability level   ____   ____   ____   ____

    i. use my own judgment   ____   ____   ____   ____

    j. Others? Please specify. _____   ____   ____   ____   ____

3. How frequently do you use the following *testing methods* to see if a textbook's reading level is suitable for your students' instruction? (Please make *one* choice for *each* method.)

TO TRY OUT TEXTBOOKS, I USE	Always	Often	Seldom	Never
a. cloze tests	____	____	____	____
b. multiple-choice tests	____	____	____	____
c. oral reading tests	____	____	____	____

COMMENTS ON TECHNIQUES OR TESTING METHODS USED FOR DETERMINING SUITABLE READING LEVELS?

_____

_____

_____

4. Often, the numbers and reading achievement of students in instructional groups vary. Please select a *single choice* that best describes a "match" you would consider most suitable between the reading level of a textbook and the reading achievement of students in the following groups.

    a. WITH A GROUP OF 2 TO 9 STUDENTS, I would match the textbook reading level to the reading level of: (Check one)

        ____ higher achieving students.

        ____ middle achieving students.

        ____ lower achieving students.

    b. WITH A GROUP OF 10 TO 19 STUDENTS, I would match the textbook reading level to the reading level of: (Check one)

        ____ higher achieving students.

        ____ middle achieving students.

        ____ lower achieving students.

    c. WITH A GROUP OF 20 OR MORE STUDENTS, I would match the textbook reading level to the reading level of: (Check one)

        ____ higher achieving students.

        ____ middle achieving students.

        ____ lower achieving students.

5. Suppose you are selecting a textbook for an individual student whose reading achievement level you know. Please select a *single choice* from the five on the right below

that best describes a "match" you would recommend as most suitable between students with high, middle, and low achievement levels and a textbook reading level.

STUDENT ACHIEVEMENT LEVELS	TEXTBOOK READING LEVELS				
	Much Higher	Somewhat Higher	The Same	Somewhat Lower	Much Lower
a. High	_____	_____	_____	_____	_____
b. Middle	_____	_____	_____	_____	_____
c. Low	_____	_____	_____	_____	_____

COMMENTS ON TEXTBOOK SELECTION FOR GROUPS AND INDIVIDUAL STUDENTS?

_____

_____

_____

THANK YOU FOR YOUR ASSISTANCE!!!

(A similar form was sent to elementary school teachers.)

APPENDIX B

Textbooks and Other Materials Surveyed

APPENDIX B–1
Social Studies and Science Textbooks Recommended by Educational Publishers

The following list of textbooks in social studies and science was used in the comparative analysis reported on in Chapter 5.

TEXTBOOKS PUBLISHED BETWEEN 1974 AND 1982

Social Studies: Grade 4

Allyn & Bacon, *Agriculture: People and the Land*, 1975
Allyn & Bacon, *Industry: People and the Machine*, 1975
Allyn & Bacon, *Journey Through Many Lands*, 1981
Allyn & Bacon, *Journey Through the Americas*, 1981
Follett, *Exploring Our World: Regions*, 1980
Ginn, *The People*, 1982
Harcourt Brace Jovanovich, *The Earth*, 1982
Laidlaw, *Understanding Regions of the Earth*, 1981
Macmillan, *The Earth and Its People*, 1982
Scholastic, *Our Country Today*, 1981

Social Studies: Grade 8

Allyn & Bacon, *Our America*, 1977
Globe, *Exploring American History*, 1981
Harcourt Brace Jovanovich, *America: Its People and Values*, 1979

Heath, *We The People*, 1982
Houghton Mifflin, *This Is America's Story*, 1981
Laidlaw, *Two Centuries of Progress*, 1981
Rand McNally, *The Free and the Brave*, 1980
Scott, Foresman, *America! America!*, 1977

Social Studies: Grade 11

Follett, *American History*, 1979
Ginn, *American History for Today*, 1974
Ginn, *History of the United States*, 1981
Globe, *Exploring Our Nation's History*, 1979
Harcourt Brace Jovanovich, *Rise of the American Nation*, 1982
Heath, *American Pageant*, 1979
Macmillan, *History of a Free People*, 1981

Science: Grade 4

Ginn, *Elementary Science 4*, 1980
Harcourt Brace Jovanovich, *Concepts in Science*, 1980
Heath, *Heath Science*, 1981
Laidlaw, *Exploring Science*, 1979
McGraw-Hill, *Reading About Science D*, 1981
McGraw-Hill, *Reading About Science E*, 1981
Merrill, *Accent on Science*, 1980
Silver Burdett, *Science: Understanding Your Environment*, 1981

Science: Grade 8

American Book, *Earth Science*, 1978
Cebco, *Concepts and Challenges in Physical Science*, 1978
Harcourt Brace Jovanovich, *Energy: A Physical Science*, 1980
Holt, Rinehart and Winston, *Modern Physical Science*, 1979
Merrill, *Focus on Physical Science*, 1981
Prentice-Hall, *Introductory Physical Science*, 1982
Prentice-Hall, *Physical Science*, 1981

Science: Grade 11

Globe, *Concepts in Modern Chemistry*, 1982
Heath, *Chemistry: Experiments and Principles*, 1982
Heath, *Problem Solving in Experimental Chemistry*, 1981
Holt, Rinehart and Winston, *Action Chemistry*, 1979

Merrill, *Chemistry: A Modern Course*, 1979
Prentice-Hall, *Chemistry: Experimental Foundations*, 1982

TEXTBOOKS PUBLISHED BETWEEN 1985 AND 1989

Social Studies: Grade 4

Harcourt Brace Jovanovich, *States and Regions*, 1988
Heath, *Regions Far and Near*, 1987
Silver Burdett & Ginn, *Geography of States and Regions*, 1988

Social Studies: Grade 8

Harcourt Brace Jovanovich, *America: Its People and Values*, 1985
Heath, *The American People*, 1986
Silver Burdett & Ginn, *One Flag, One Land*, 1988

Social Studies: Grade 11

Harcourt Brace Jovanovich, *Triumph of the American Nation*, 1986
Prentice-Hall, *A History of the United States Since 1861*, 1989
Prentice-Hall, *The United States: A History of the Republic*, 1988

Science: Grade 4

Harcourt Brace Jovanovich, *Harcourt Science*, 1985
Macmillan, *Journeys into Science*, 1988
Merrill, *Merrill Science*, 1989
Silver Burdett & Ginn, *Silver Science*, 1989

Science: Grade 8

Heath, *Physical Science*, 1987
Macmillan, *Earth Science*, 1989
Merrill, *Focus on Earth Science*, 1989
Silver Burdett & Ginn, *General Science*, 1989

Science: Grade 11

Heath, *Heath Chemistry*, 1987
Heath, *Heath Physics*, 1986
Merrill, *Chemistry: A Modern Course*, 1987
Merrill, *Physics: Principles and Problems*, 1986

APPENDIX B–2
Reading and Content-Area Methods Textbooks

READING METHODS TEXTBOOKS
PUBLISHED BETWEEN 1950 AND 1980

Austin, M. C., & Morrison, C. (1963). *The first R: The Harvard report on reading.* New York: Macmillan.

Barbe, W. B. (1961). *Educator's guide to personalized reading instruction.* Englewood Cliffs, NJ: Prentice-Hall.

Berry, A., Barrett, T. C., & Powell, R. (1969). *Elementary reading instruction: Selected materials.* Needham Heights, MA: Allyn and Bacon.

Bond, G. L., & Wagner, E. B.(1950). *Teaching the child to read* (rev. ed.). New York: Macmillan.

Carter, H. L. J., & McGinnis, D. J. (1962). *Teaching individuals to read.* Lexington, MA: D. C. Heath.

Durkin, D. (1970). *Teaching them to read.* Needham Heights, MA: Allyn & Bacon.

Durkin, D. (1974). *Teaching them to read* (2nd ed.). Boston: Allyn & Bacon.

Durkin, D. (1978). *Teaching them to read* (3rd ed.). Boston: Allyn & Bacon.

Farr, R., & Roser, N. (1979). *Teaching a child to read.* New York: Harcourt Brace Jovanovich.

Fry, E. (1972). *Reading instruction for classroom and clinic.* New York: McGraw-Hill.

Fry, E. (1977). *Elementary reading instruction.* New York: McGraw-Hill.

Guszak, F. J. (1978). *Diagnostic reading instruction in the elementary school* (2nd ed.). New York: Harper & Row.

Hall, M. A., Ribovich, J. K., & Ramig, C. J. (1979). *Reading and the elementary school child* (2nd ed.). New York: D. Van Nostrand.

Harris, A. J. (1970). *How to increase reading ability* (5th ed.). New York: David McKay.

Harris, A. J., & Sipay, E. R. (1980). *How to increase reading ability.* New York: Longman.

Harris, L., & Smith, C. (1976). *Reading instruction.* New York: Holt, Rinehart and Winston.

Heilman, A. W. (1967). *Principles and practices of teaching reading* (2nd ed.). Columbus, OH: Charles E. Merrill.

Hester, K. B. (1955). *Teaching every child to read* (2nd ed.). New York: Harper & Brothers.

Hildreth, G. (1958). *Teaching reading*. New York: Holt, Rinehart and Winston.

Karlin, R. (1980). *Teaching elementary reading (principles and strategies)* (3rd ed.). New York: Harcourt Brace Jovanovich.

McCracken, G. (1959). *The right to learn*. Chicago: Henry Regnery.

McKim, M. G. (1955). *Guiding growth in reading in the modern elementary school*. New York: Macmillan.

Olson, J. P., & Dillner, M. H. (1976). *Learning to teach reading in the elementary school*. New York: Macmillan.

Otto, W., Rude, R., & Spiegel, D. L. (1979). *How to teach reading*. Reading, MA: Addison-Wesley.

Ruddell, R. B. (1974). *Reading-language instruction: Innovative practices*. Englewood Cliffs, NJ: Prentice-Hall.

Spache, G. (1963). *Toward better reading*. Champaign, IL: Garrard.

Veatch, J., & Acinapuro, P. J. (1968). *Reading in the elementary school*. New York: Ronald Press.

Walcutt, L., & M'cracken. (1974). *Teaching reading — A phonic/linguistic approach to developmental reading*. New York: Macmillan.

Yoakam, G. A. (1955). *Basal reading instruction*. New York: McGraw-Hill.

READING METHODS TEXTBOOKS
PUBLISHED BETWEEN 1984 AND 1988

Burnes, P. C., Roe, B. D., & Ross, E. P. (1988). *Teaching reading in today's elementary schools*. Boston: Houghton Mifflin.

Finn, P. J. (1985). *Helping children learn to read*. New York: Random House.

Harris, A. J., & Sipay, E. R. (1984). *How to increase reading ability*. New York: Longman.

Heilman, A. W., Blair, T. R., & Rupley, W. H. (1986). *Principles and practices of teaching reading*. Columbus, OH: Charles E. Merrill.

Mason, J. M., & Au, K. H. (1986). *Reading instruction for today*. Glenview, IL: Scott, Foresman.

Vacca, J. L., Vacca, R. T., & Gove, M. K. (1987). *Reading and learning to read*. Boston: Little, Brown.

SOCIAL STUDIES AND SCIENCE METHODS TEXTBOOKS

Banks, J. A. (1977). *Teaching strategies for the social studies — Inquiry, valuing, and decision-making*. Reading, MA: Addison-Wesley.

Blough, G. O., & Hugget, A. J. (1951). *Elementary school science and how to teach it*. New York: Dryden Press.

Blough, G. O., & Schwartz, J. (1969). *Elementary school science and how to teach it* (4th ed.). New York: Holt, Rinehart & Winston.

Blough, G. O., & Schwartz, J. (1974). *Elementary school science and how to teach it* (5th ed.). New York: Holt, Rinehart and Winston.

Blough, G. O., Schwartz, J., & Huggett, A. J. (1958). *Elementary school science and how to teach it* (rev. ed.). Hinsdale, IL: Dryden Press.

Clark, L. H. (1973). *Teaching social studies in secondary schools — A handbook*. New York: Macmillan.

Ehman, L., Mehlinger, H., & Patrick, J. (1974). *Toward effective instruction in secondary social studies*. Boston: Houghton Mifflin.

Ester, W. K. (1973). *Teaching elementary science*. Belmont, CA: Wadsworth.

Hone, J. V. (1962). *A sourcebook for elementary science*. New York: Harcourt, Brace and World.

Hone, J. V. (1971). *A sourcebook for elementary science*. New York: Harcourt, Brace and World.

Hunt, M. P., & Metcalf, L. E. (1968). *Teaching high school social studies*. New York: Harper & Row.

Jarolimek, J. (1959). *Social studies in elementary education*. New York: Macmillan.

Jarolimek, J. (1963). *Social studies in elementary education* (2nd ed.). New York: Macmillan.

Jarolimek, J. (1967). *Social studies in elementary education* (3rd ed.). New York: Macmillan.

Jarolimek, J. (1971). *Social studies in elementary education* (4th ed.). New York: Macmillan.

Leinwand, G., & Feins, D. M. (1968). *Teaching history and social studies in secondary schools*. Aulander, NC: Pittman.

Lewenstein, M. R. (1963). *Teaching social studies in junior and senior high school*. Chicago: Rand McNally.

Martorella, P. H. (1976). *Elementary social studies as a learning system*. New York: Harper & Row.

Merritt, E. (1961). *Working with children in social studies*. Belmont, CA: Wadsworth.

Michaels, J. V. (1950). *Social studies for children in a democracy*. Englewood Cliffs, NJ: Prentice-Hall.

Renner, J. W., & Stafford, D. G. (1979). *Teaching science in elementary school*. New York: Harper & Row.

Selberg, E. M., Nael, L. A., & Vessel, M. F. (1970). *Discovering science in elementary school*. Reading, MA: Addison-Wesley.

Sistrunk, W. E., & Matson, R. C. (1972). *A practical approach to secondary social studies*. Dubuque, IA: William C. Brown.

APPENDIX B–3
Books and Articles on Textbooks: 1985–1989

Armbruster, B., Osborn, J., & Davison, A. (1985). Readability formulas may be dangerous to your textbooks. *Educational Leadership*, *42*:7, 18–20.

Cannon, P. (1989). Readability formulas: An update. *Social Studies Review*, *1*, 8–9.

Farr, R., & Tulley, M. (1985). Do adoption committees perpetuate mediocre textbooks? *Phi Delta Kappan*, *66*:7, 467–471.

Goodman, K., Shannon, P., Freeman, Y., & Murphy, S. (1988). *Report card on basal readers*. Katonah, NY: Richard C. Owen Publishers.

Grundin, H. (1989). *If it ain't whole it ain't language*. Talk delivered to the Association of American Publishers, Chicago, IL.

Nagel, K., & Woodward, A. (1989). Elementary grade textbooks: A case of overskill. *Social Studies Review*, *1*, 5–8.

Osborn, J., Jones, B., & Stein, M. (1985). The case for improving textbooks. *Educational Leadership*, *42*:7, 9–16.

Sewall, G. (1987). *American history textbooks*. New York: Educational Excellence Network.

Sewall, G. (1988). Literacy lackluster. *American Educator*, Spring, 32–37.

Stahl, S. (1989). *Response to "whole language"* (Response to Hans Grundin). Talk delivered to the Association of American Publishers, Chicago, IL.

Tyson-Bernstein, H. (1988). The academy's contribution to the impoverishment of America's textbooks. *Phi Delta Kappan*, 193–198.

Tyson-Bernstein, H., & Woodward, A. (1989). Nineteenth century policies for 21st century practice: The textbook reform dilemma. *Educational Policy*, *3*:2, 95–106.

APPENDIX B–4
Instructional Materials for Social Studies, Science, and Reading
Used in the Elementary- and Secondary-Level Classrooms Observed

SOCIAL STUDIES: GRADE 4

Follett, *Exploring Our World: Regions* (Follett Social Studies), 1980
Follett, *The World of Mankind* (The Environments We Live In Series), 1973
Macmillan, *Our Country and Other Lands* (Macmillan Social Studies), 1980
Marblehead Public School Teachers, *Tribute to Marblehead*, no date
Singer, *Man Changes His World* (2nd ed.), 1967

SOCIAL STUDIES: GRADE 6

Follett, *Exploring Our World: Eastern Hemisphere*, 1977
Follett, *Exploring Regions of the Eastern Hemisphere*, 1971
Ginn, *Our World Inquiring and Learning* (new ed.; The Tiegs-Adams Studies), 1975
Macmillan, *Living in the Old World* (Macmillan Social Studies Series), 1969
Macmillan, *The Old World* (Macmillan Social Studies), 1980
Scott, Foresman, *Scott, Foresman Social Studies*, 1979

SOCIAL STUDIES: GRADE 8

Harcourt Brace Jovanovich, *American Civics* (2nd ed.), 1974
Harcourt Brace Jovanovich, *The Rise of the American Nation* (2nd ed.), 1966
Houghton Mifflin, *This Is America's Story*, 1966
Marblehead Public Schools, *American Revolution Unit*, no date
Marblehead Public Schools, *Life Aboard a Whaler*, no date
Rand McNally, *The Free and the Brave: The Story of the American People* (2nd ed.), 1972

SOCIAL STUDIES: GRADE 11

Cambridge Books, *Patterns of Civilization*, 1973
Harcourt Brace Jovanovich, *Rise of the American Nation* (Heritage ed.), 1977
Harcourt, Brace & World, *Major Crises in American History: Documentary Problems*, 1962
Harcourt, Brace & World, *The National Experience*, 1966
Laidlaw, *A High School History of Modern America*, 1977
Macmillan, *Background for Tomorrow: An American History*, 1965
Macmillan, *History of a Free People*, 1978
Macmillan, *Modern Times*, 1966
Sadlier-Oxford, *Mainstreams of World History*, 1975
Scholastic, *American Adventures*, 1979

SCIENCE: GRADE 4

Harcourt Brace Jovanovich, *Concepts in Science* (Newton ed.), 1975
Heath, *Science in Your Life* (Heath Elementary Science 4), 1959
Marblehead Public Schools, *Animals Unit*, no date
Marblehead Public Schools, *Food Unit*, no date
Marblehead Public Schools, *Notes on Tidepools*, no date
McGraw-Hill, *Gateways to Science*, 1979
Merrill, *Accent on Science 4*, 1980

SCIENCE: GRADE 6

Ginn, *Experimenting in Science*, 1955
Globe, *Pathways in Science 1, Physics: The Forces of Nature*, 1975
Globe, *Pathways in Science 2, Chemistry: Of Mixtures*, 1975
Harcourt Brace Jovanovich, *Concepts in Science* (Newton ed.), 1975
Heath, *Science for Today and Tomorrow, 6*, 1965
Laidlaw, *Health for Living* (2nd ed.), 1977
Milliken, *Milliken Science Duplication Masters*, 1966
Winston, *The New Discovering Why*, 1956

SCIENCE: GRADE 8

Current Science, September 9, 1981; and October 7, 1981
Merrill, *Focus on Earth Science* (2nd ed.), 1972

Prentice-Hall, *Introductory Physical Science*, 1972
Scholastic Science World, February 6, 1981; and October 16, 1981
Silver Burdett, *The Natural World/2*, 1976

SCIENCE: GRADE 11

Center for Personalized Instruction, *PSSC Workbook*, 1975
Heath, *PSSC Physics*, 1971
Holt, Rinehart & Winston, *Action Chemistry*, 1979
Holt, Rinehart & Winston, *Foundations of Chemistry*, 1973
Holt, Rinehart & Winston, *Modern Chemistry*, 1978
Merrill, *Focus on Science Series*, 1976

READING: GRADE 4

American, *Catching Glimpses*, 1980
American, *Clearing Paths*, 1980
American, *Crossing Boundaries*, 1980
Ginn, *The Dog Next Door and Other Stories* (Rainbow ed.), 1980
Ginn, *How It Is Nowadays* (Rainbow ed.), 1980
Ginn, *Inside Out* (Rainbow ed.), 1980
Harcourt Brace Jovanovich, *Ring Around the World* (The Bookmark Reading Program: Primary Readers), 1970
Houghton Mifflin, *Images*, 1973
Houghton Mifflin, *Kaleidoscope*, 1971
Lippincott, *Soaring* (Basic Reading: Book J), 1978
Lippincott, *Taking Off* (Basic Reading: Book I), 1978
Macmillan, *Better Than Gold* (Macmillan Reading Program), 1965

READING: GRADES 4 AND 6

Ginn, *A Lizard to Start With* (Rainbow ed.), 1980

READING: GRADE 6

Allyn and Bacon, *Study Skills for Information Retrieval*, 1974
Field Enterprises, *Thunderbolts* (Field Literature Program), 1971
Ginn, *Measure Me, Sky* (Rainbow ed.), 1980
Ginn, *Mountains Are for Climbing* (Rainbow ed.), 1980

Ginn, *Tell Me How the Sun Rose* (Rainbow ed.), 1980
Houghton Mifflin, *Galaxies*, 1971
Houghton Mifflin, *Networks*, 1979
Lippincott, *Reading for Meaning: A Program for Improving Reading*, 1955
Lowell & Lynwood, *Multiple Skills Series* (E 1), 1976
McGraw-Hill, *New Practice Readers* (Book D), 1962
Rand McNally, *The New Phonics We Use* (Book G), 1972
Reader's Digest, *New Reading Skill Builder*, 1967
Scott, Foresman, *Reading Tactics A*, 1977

READING: GRADE 8

American, *Meeting Challenges*, 1980
Amsco, *Stories from the 4 Corners*, 1975
Amsco, *Stories to Teach and Delight*, 1977
Ginn, *To Make a Difference* (Rainbow ed.), 1978
Ginn, *Windows and Walls* (Rainbow ed.), 1980
Midwest, *Critical Thinking Book 2*, 1980
Prentice-Hall, *Be a Better Reader* (Level E, Basic Skills ed.), 1978
Reader's Digest, *Reader's Digest Adventure*, no date
Scott, Foresman, *Tactics in Reading I: Basic Reading Skills*, 1965

APPENDIX C

Student Survey Instruments

APPENDIX C-1
Procedures for Student Testing and Interviewing

I. For the Administration of the Cloze Test (maximum of 6 students):
   1. Explain the purpose of the study to the students.
   2. Ask students if they want to participate in the study.
   3. Determine the name of the textbooks used by each student to insure that the correct cloze passage is given to each student.
   4. Present the 3 cloze passages to each student, shuffled in order, and then stapled.
   5. Read the direction for the cloze test orally with the students, doing the examples together.
   6. Give students unlimited time to complete the testing.

II. For Oral Interviews (of one student at a time):
   1. Review the purpose of the study with the student.
   2. Explain the procedures of the interview to the student, stressing that the student is expected to be critical and negative if the passage warrants this. Give the student permission to be critical and negative, as an editor would be.
   3. Ask the student if he or she wants to participate in the interview.
   4. Shuffle the oral reading passages so that they are handed to the student out of order.
   5. Ask the student to read the first passage orally. Keep track of all oral reading errors and level of reading fluency on the interviewer's copy of the passage. Self-corrections are not considered to be errors, but do affect fluency.
   6. Ask the student the questions concerning the passage (given in the interview schedule). Write the responses on the interview

schedule. The student may look at the passage while answering questions for all questions except number 3, where it is explicitly stated not to look at the passage.

7. Repeat procedures 5 and 6 for all three passages (one for reading, one for social studies, and one for science, in any order).

APPENDIX C–2
Directions for Cloze Passages

[*These instructions are to be read aloud, with students following along.*]

On each of the following 3 pages, you will find a reading passage taken from your school textbooks. Words have been left out of the passages and blanks have been put in their places. *Your job is to guess what word was left out and write that word in the blank, for each blank.* Reading the whole passage first can help you decide what word goes in each blank.

It will help you to remember these things:

1. Write only *one* word in each blank.
2. Try and fill every blank. It is O.K. to guess.
3. You may have to skip the hard ones and then go back to them when you have finished.
4. Do not worry about spelling, as long as we can tell what word you mean.

Practice examples:

A. "Good morning, class," _____ the teacher.
B. We will go for a ride _____ our car.

APPENDIX C–3
Student Interview Schedule

Student identification number ____   Interviewer_____

School code ____   Date of interview _____

STUDENT INFORMATION:

Sex: ___boy ___girl   Age: 8 9 10 11 12 13 14 15   Grade: 4 6 8

Reading level as judged by teacher: below average   average   above average

TESTED READING ACHIEVEMENT:

Test name _____   Date given _____   Raw score _____

Reading grade-equivalent level _____   Percentile _____   Stanine _____

ADJUSTED READING ACHIEVEMENT TEST SCORE FOR EQUIVALENCE TO DATE OF INTERVIEW:

Adjusted reading grade-equivalent level: _____

1st Passage: (Student reads passage orally to interviewer.)

a. Subject of passage: reading lesson   social studies   science

b. Readability level of passage: raw score _____   corrected grade level _____

c. Relation of passage readability level to student's tested reading achievement level:

| passage is much easier | passage is slightly easier | passage is the same | passage is slightly harder | passage is much harder |

d. Level of student's reading fluency and expresison when reading the passage:

| very halting with poor expression | slightly halting | slightly fluent | very fluent with good expression |

e. Number of student's oral reading errors when reading the passage (do not include self-corrections or repetitions, or insignificant errors such as *a* for *the*):

Total number of errors: _____
Percentage of total errors in relation to total words in passage: _____

f. Questions asked of student about this passage:

   1. Without looking at the passage, what important things did you learn from reading it that you would tell a friend? (This question should be probed.)

   2. Now look at the passage, what else would you tell a friend about it?

3. How easy or hard did you think this passage was for you to understand?

| much too easy | too easy | just about right | too hard | much too hard |

4. What makes you say that?

5. If you could choose, in order to learn a lot about [reading/social studies/science], would you want the school books that you use during a lesson with your teacher to be harder, or easier, or the same as this passage?

        harder   the same   easier

6. What makes you say that?

7. Also, if you could choose, when you are asked to work from your school books by yourself without any help from your teacher, would you want your school books to be harder, or easier, or the same as this passage?

        harder   the same   easier

8. What makes you say that?

9. What could be done to change this passage to make it better for you to learn from?

10. How well do you like this passage?

  I like it a lot   I like it   It's O.K.   I don't like it   I don't like it at all

11. What makes you say that?

APPENDIX D

Evaluation Criteria for Books

APPENDIX D–1
Question Complexity Rating Scale

The question complexity rating scale, based on Bloom's *Taxonomy of Educational Objectives* (1956), was adapted from a scale developed by Chall, Conard, and Harris (1977). The scale defines four levels of question complexity for judging and numerically rating the difficulty of questions in textbooks and workbooks. Definitions of the four levels of question complexity follow.

Level One.   Questions that require recall and reiteration of facts. These questions ask students to name people or dates in history, recall specific facts stated in text, and define vocabulary words. Most often these questions involve answering true/false, multiple-choice, and fill-in-the-blank questions. Some examples of factual questions are:

What are two major types of transportation people use on the tundra?

Determine whether each of the following sentences is true or false.
1. Silver chloride is soluble in water.
2. In ordinary chemical reactions, no mass is lost.

What types of corruption appeared at the state and federal levels?

Level Two.   Questions that require summarizing main ideas, describing processes, and making inferences. These questions usually involve the integration of factual information presented in text. Some examples of integrative questions are:

How did the Eskimos use their natural environment to meet their basic needs?

Some people at the end of the 19th century thought cities were wonderful
   places to live. Other people felt they were not. Choose two of the
   following people and write a short paragraph explaining what each
   person might have thought about city life and why:
   a. a rich society leader
   b. a recent immigrant in a poor neighborhood
   c. a social worker at a settlement house
   d. a suburban commuter

Why are formulas not changed when balancing equations?

   Level Three.   Questions that require students to compare and contrast
different points of view, physical objects, events in history, and lifestyles
and environments. Examples of compare-and-contrast questions are:

How does Ar-luk and Nik's house differ from modern Alaskan homes?

Reread the selection on pages 441–442 describing John Rockefeller's comments on the South Improvement Co. to the owner of a small refinery.
   Pretend you are that reluctant owner. Write a letter to Mr. Rockefeller
   denying his request.

How does plasma differ from the other three states of matter?

   Level Four.   Questions that require readers to justify and support their
answers. To answer these questions, readers must not only understand the
information presented in the text, but they must decide what key elements
best justify their answer. Readers, therefore, must think critically to answer such questions. Examples of critical questions are:

"The Open Door was designed primarily to promote U.S. trade rather than
   China's rights." Is this a valid statement? Explain.

Compare the vote in the House with that in the Senate and account for the
   differences.

Did the Eskimos of long ago have a simple or complex level of technology?
   Explain your answer.

APPENDIX D–2
Chall's Stages of Reading Development

The following stages indicate the reading maturity required by various reading materials.

Stage 1 (Grades 1, 2). Reading that is primarily associating written words to words in the child's oral vocabulary. Materials are simple text that contains high frequency words and words that are phonetically regular.

Stage 2 (Grades 2, 3). Reading to confirm what is already known. Energy is still mainly concentrated on decoding words and developing fluency in reading connected text. Therefore the vocabulary is generally within the reader's meaning vocabulary, although not all words need be immediately recognizable.

Stage 3A (Grades 4 to 6). Reading for new knowledge, generally from one viewpoint; facts, concepts, how to do things. The reader is also learning a process—how to find information in a paragraph, chapter, book. This stage does not usually require special knowledge to understand the text, but subjects studied in school are generally introduced at this stage. Materials include subject-matter textbooks, trade books, reference works, newspapers, magazines, more complex fiction and non-fiction. Vocabulary goes beyond the elemental and common and is increasingly unfamiliar, i.e., learned from books in school.

Stage 3B (Grades 7 to 8). Tasks and characteristics of Stage 3B are similar to those of Stage 3A, but the reader reacts more critically to the text than in Stage 3A. The language of texts becomes more complex in syntax and abstract in vocabulary.

Stage 4 (High School). This stage is characterized by reading from multiple viewpoints. The reader must deal with more than one set of facts, theories, and viewpoints in arriving at a critical synthesis and analysis of the material. A broad range of materials is used, including both expository and narrative writing. Topics and language are complex, specialized, literary, etc., including physical and biological sciences, humanities, high quality and popular literature. Newspapers and magazines provide divergent views.

Stage 5 (College and beyond).   The reader constructs knowledge on a high level of abstraction and generality. Past knowledge about the subject and broad general knowledge are needed for full comprehension of the text. The topics and language of the text are the most difficult, abstract, and general. This stage is characterized by wide reading of the most difficult materials.

Source: Chall, J. S. (1983). *Stages of reading development.* New York: McGraw-Hill.

References

Anderson, T., & Armbruster, B. (1984). Content area textbooks. In R. Anderson, J. Osborn, & R. Tierney (Eds.), *Learning to read in American schools: Basal readers and content textbooks* (pp. 193–226). Hillsdale, NJ: Lawrence Erlbaum Associates.

Applebee, A. N., Langer, J. A., & Mullis, I. V. S. (1989). *Crossroads in American education*. Princeton, NJ: Educational Testing Service, and National Assessment of Educational Progress.

Armbruster, B. (1984). The problem of inconsiderate text. In G. Duffy, L. Roehler, & J. Mason (Eds.), *Comprehension instruction* (pp. 202–217). New York: Longman.

Armbruster, B. B., Osborn, J. H., & Davison, A. L. (1985). Readability formulas may be dangerous to your textbooks. *Educational Leadership, 42*(7), 18–20.

Bartlett, F. (1932). *Remembering*. Cambridge, England: Cambridge University Press.

Betts, E. (1946). *Foundations of reading instruction*. New York: American Book Company.

Black, H. (1967). *The American schoolbook*. New York: William Morrow.

Bloom, B. (1956). *Taxonomy of educational objectives: Cognitive domain*. New York: David McKay.

Bloom, B. (1964). *Stability and change in human characteristics*. New York: John Wiley.

Bloom, B. (1976). *Human characteristics and school learning*. New York: McGraw-Hill.

Bormuth, J. R. (1967). Comparing cloze and multiple-choice comprehension test scores. *Journal of Reading, 10*, 291–299.

Bormuth, J. R. (1969, March). *Development of readability analyses* (Final Report, Project No. 7-0052, Contract No. 1, OEC-3-7-070552-0362). Washington, DC: Department of Health, Education, and Welfare, Office of Education.

Bormuth, J. R. (1971). *Development of standards of readability* (Project No. 9-0237). Washington, DC: U.S. Department of Health, Education, and Welfare. (ERIC Document Reproduction Service No. ED 054 233)

Bormuth, J. R. (1975). Reading literacy: Its definitions and assessment. In J. Carroll & J. Chall (Eds.), *Toward a literate society* (pp. 61–100). New York: McGraw-Hill.

Bruner, J. (1960). *The process of education*. Cambridge, MA: Harvard University Press.

151

Bruner, J. (1966). *Toward a theory of instruction*. Cambridge, MA: Harvard University Press.

Carroll, J. (1963). A model of school learning. *Teachers College Record, 64*, 723–732.

Carver, R. (1975–1976). Measuring prose difficulty using the Rauding scale. *Reading Research Quarterly, 11*, 660–685.

Chall, J. S. (1947). This business of readability. *Educational Research Bulletin, 26*(1), 1–13.

Chall, J. S. (1958). *Readability: An appraisal of research and application*. Columbus: Ohio State University Press.

Chall, J. S. (1967). *Learning to read: The great debate*. New York: McGraw-Hill.

Chall, J. S. (1983a). *Learning to read: The great debate* (updated ed.). New York: McGraw-Hill.

Chall, J. S. (1983b). *Stages of reading development*. New York: McGraw-Hill.

Chall, J. S. (1984). Readability and prose comprehension: Continuities and discontinuities. In J. Flood (Ed.), *Understanding reading comprehension* (pp. 233–246). Newark, DE: International Reading Association.

Chall, J. S. (1988). The beginning years. In B. Zakaluk & S. J. Samuels (Eds.), *Readability: Its past, present, and future* (pp. 2–13). Newark, DE: International Reading Association.

Chall, J. S. (1989). *Learning to read: The great debate* 20 years later: A response to "Debunking the great phonics myths." *Phi Delta Kappan, 70*, 521–538.

Chall, J. S., Bissex, G., Conard, S., & Harris-Sharples, S. (in press). *Holistic assessment of text: Scales for estimating the difficulty of literature, social studies and science materials*. Boston: Houghton Mifflin.

Chall, J. S., & Conard, S. (1984). Resources and their use for reading instruction. In A. Purves & O. Niles (Eds.), *Becoming readers in a complex society* (pp. 209–232). Chicago: National Society for the Study of Education.

Chall, J. S., Conard, S., & Harris, S. (1977, June). *An analysis of textbooks in relation to declining SAT scores*. Princeton, NJ: College Entrance Examination Board, and Educational Testing Service.

Chall, J. S., Jacobs, V. A., & Baldwin, L. E. (1990). *The reading crisis: Why poor children fall behind*. Cambridge, MA: Harvard University Press.

Chall, J. S., & Squire, J. R. (1991). The publishing industry and textbooks. In R. Barr, M. Kamil, P. Mosenthal, & P. D. Pearson (Eds.), *Handbook of reading research* (Vol. 2, pp. 120–146). White Plains, NY: Longman.

Clark, C. (1981). Assessing comprehensibility: The PHAN system. *Reading Teacher, 34*, 670–675.

Clifford, G. J. (1978). Words for schools: The applications in education of the vocabulary researches of Edward L. Thorndike. In P. Suppes (Ed.), *Impact of research on education: Some case studies* (pp. 107–198). Washington, DC: National Academy of Education.

Cody, C. (Ed.). (1986). *A policymaker's guide to textbook selection*. Alexandria, VA: National Association of State Boards of Education.

College Entrance Examination Board. (1979, 1980). *Degrees of reading power*. New York: Author.

College Entrance Examination Board. (1977). *On further examination: Report of the Advisory Panel on the Scholastic Aptitude Test score decline.* New York: Author.

Conard, S. (1984). *On readability and readability formula scores* (Occasional Paper). Lexington, MA: Ginn and Company.

Dale, E., & Chall, J. S. (1948). A formula for predicting readability. *Educational Research Bulletin, 27*(1), 11–20; (2), 37–54.

Dale, E., & Chall, J. S. (in press). *Readability revisited and the new Dale-Chall readability formula.* Boston: Houghton Mifflin.

Davison, A., & Green, G. (Eds.). (1988). *Linguistic complexity and text comprehension: Readability issues reconsidered.* Hillsdale, NJ: Lawrence Erlbaum Associates.

Dolch, E. (1928). Combined word studies. *Journal of Educational Research, 17,* 11–19.

Durkin, D. (1978–1979). What classroom observations reveal about comprehension instruction. *Reading Research Quarterly, 14,* 481–533.

Durkin, D. (1984). Is there a match between what elementary teachers do and what basal manuals recommend? *Reading Teacher, 37,* 734–744.

Education Week. (1988, September 7). Evaluating teachers' outlook on textbooks [Letter to the editor], p. 48.

Elliot, D. L., & Woodward, A. (Eds.). (1990). *Textbooks and schooling in the United States. 89th yearbook of the national society for the study of education, Part I.* Chicago: University of Chicago Press.

EPIE Institute. (1976). *National study on the nature and quality of instructional materials most used by teachers and learners.* New York: Teachers College, Columbia University.

Farr, R., & Tulley, M. A. (1985). Do adoption committees perpetuate mediocre textbooks? *Phi Delta Kappan, 66,* 467–471.

Farr, R., Tulley, M., & Powell, D. (1987). The evaluation and selection of basal readers. *Elementary School Journal, 87,* 267–282.

Farr, R., Tulley, M. A., & Rayford, L. (1987). Selecting basal readers: A comparison of school districts in adoption and non-adoption states. *Journal of Research and Development in Education, 20*(4), 59–72.

Fiske, E. (1987, August 2). The push for smarter textbooks. *The New York Times,* Section 12, pp. 20–23.

FitzGerald, F. (1979). *America revised.* New York: Vintage Books.

Flesch, R. (1950). How to test readability: Measuring the level of abstraction. *Journal of Applied Psychology, 34,* 384–390.

Freebody, P., & Anderson, R. C. (1983). Effects of vocabulary difficulty, text cohesion, and schema availability on reading comprehension. *Reading Research Quarterly, 18,* 277–294.

Freeman, D., & Porter, A. (1988, April). *Does the content of classroom instruction match the content of textbooks?* Paper presented at the annual meeting of the American Educational Research Association, New Orleans.

Fry, E. (1977, December). Fry's readability graph: Clarification, validity, and extension to level 17. *Journal of Reading, 21,* 242–252.

Fry, E. (1989). Reading formulas: Maligned but valid. *Journal of Reading, 32,* 292–297.

Gagnon, P. (1987). *Democracy's untold story: What world history textbooks neglect.* Washington, DC: American Federation of Teachers.

Gates, A. I. (1930). *Interest and ability in reading.* New York: Macmillan.

Gates, A. I. (1961). Vocabulary control in basal reading material. *Reading Teacher, 15,* 81–85.

Goodman, K., Shannon, P., Freeman, Y., & Murphy, S. (1988). *Report card on basal readers.* Katonah, NY: Richard C. Owen.

Gray, W. S., & Leary, B. E. (1935). *What makes a book readable?* Chicago: University of Chicago Press.

Halliday, M., & Hasan, R. (1976). *Cohesion in English.* London: Longman.

Hall-Quest, A. L. (1918). *The textbook: How to use and judge it.* New York: Macmillan.

Harris, A. J., & Jacobson, M. (1982). *Basic reading vocabularies.* New York: Macmillan.

Hirsch, E. D. (1987). *Cultural literacy: What every American needs to know.* New York: Houghton Mifflin.

Hockett, J. A. (1938). The vocabularies of recent primers and first readers. *Elementary School Journal, 39,* 112–115.

Hockett, J. A., & Neeley, N. G. (1937). The vocabularies of twenty-eight first readers. *Elementary School Journal, 37,* 344–352.

Hoffman, J. V., & Roser, N. (Eds.). (1987, January). The basal reader in American reading instruction [Special issue]. *Elementary School Journal, 87*(3).

Horn, E. (1937). *Methods of instruction in the social studies* (Report of the Commission on the Social Studies, Part 15). New York: Scribner's.

Jackson, P. W., & Haroutunian-Gordon, S. (Eds.). (1989). *From Socrates to software: The teacher as text and the text as teacher. 88th yearbook of the national society for the study of education,* Part I. Chicago: University of Chicago Press.

Kamhi, M. M. (1981). *Limiting what students shall read* (Summary report on the survey *Book and materials selection for school libraries and classrooms: Procedures, challenges, and responses,* sponsored by the Association of American Publishers, the American Library Association, and the Association for Supervision and Curriculum Development). New York: Association of American Publishers. (ERIC Document Reproduction Service No. ED 210 771).

Kemper, S. (1983). Measuring the inference load of a text. *Journal of Educational Psychology, 75,* 391–401.

Kintsch, W. E., & Miller, J. (1984). Readability: A view from cognitive psychology. In J. Flood (Ed.), *Understanding reading comprehension.* Newark, DE: International Reading Association.

Kintsch, W. E., & Vipond, D. (1979). Reading comprehension and readability in educational practice and psychological theory. In L. G. Nilsson (Ed.), *Perspectives on memory research* (pp. 329–365). Hillsdale, NJ: Lawrence Erlbaum Associates.

Klare, G. (1963). *The measurement of readability.* Ames: Iowa State University Press.

Klare, G. (1974–1975). Assessing readability. *Reading Research Quarterly, 10,* 62–102.

Klare, G. R. (1979). *Readability standards for army-wide publications* (Evaluation Report No. 79-1). Fort Benjamin Harrison, IN: U.S. Army Administration Center, Directorate of Evaluation.

Klare, G. (1984). Readability. In P. D. Pearson (Ed.), *Handbook of Reading Research* (pp. 681–744). New York: Longman.

Klare, G. (1988). The formative years. In B. Zakaluk & S. J. Samuels (Eds.), *Readability: Its past, present, and future* (pp. 14–20). Newark, DE: International Reading Association.

Komoski, P. K. (1978). The realities of choosing and using instructional materials. *Educational Leadership, 36,* 46–50.

Lively, B., & Pressey, S. W. (1923). A method of measuring the vocabulary burden of textbooks. *Educational Administration and Supervision, 9,* 389–398.

Lowe, A. (1979). ThUS: A non-formula readability test. *Reading Improvement, 16,* 155–157.

McNally, D. (1973). *Piaget, education and teaching.* Sussex, England: New Educational Press.

Metropolitan Achievement Test. (1978). New York: Harcourt Brace Jovanovich.

Meyer, B. (1977). The structure of prose: Effects on learning and memory and indications for educational practice. In R. Anderson, R. Spiro, & W. Montague (Eds.), *Schooling and the acquisition of knowledge* (pp. 179–214). Hillsdale, NJ: Lawrence Erlbaum Associates.

Miller, J., & Kintsch, W. (1980). Readability and recall of short prose passages: A theoretical analysis. *Journal of Experimental Psychology: Human Learning and Memory, 6,* 335–354.

Morriss, E., & Holversen, D. (1935). *Idea analysis technique.* Unpublished paper.

Mullis, I. V. S., & Jenkins, L. B. (1990). *The reading report card, 1971–88: Trends from the nation's report card.* Princeton, NJ: Educational Testing Service, and National Assessment of Educational Progress.

National Assessment of Educational Progress. (1985). *The reading report card: Progress toward excellence in our schools.* Princeton, NJ: Educational Testing Service.

National Commission on Excellence in Education. (1983). *A nation at risk.* Washington, DC: National Institute of Education.

Piaget, J. (1952). *The origin of intelligence in children* (M. Cook, Trans.). New York: International University Press. (Original work published 1936)

Piaget, J. (1964). Development and learning. In R. Ripple & V. Rockcastle (Eds.), *Piaget rediscovered: A report of the conference on cognitive studies and curriculum development* (pp. 7–20). New York: Cornell University Department of Education.

Piaget, J. (1968). *The psychology of intelligence.* Totowa, NJ: Littlefield, Adams.

Rogers, V. (1988, August 3). School texts: The outlook of teachers. *Education Week* (Extra edition), p. 56.

Rumelhart, D. (1980). Schemata: The building blocks of cognition. In R. Spiro, B. Bruce, & W. Brewer (Eds.), *Theoretical issues in reading comprehension* (pp. 33–58). Hillsdale, NJ: Lawrence Erlbaum Associates.

Sewall, G. (1987). *American history textbooks: An assessment of quality.* New York: Columbia University, Educational Excellence Network.

Shannon, P. (1989). *Broken promises: Instruction in twentieth-century America.* Granby, MA: Bergin & Garvey.

Singer, H. (1975). The SEER technique: A non-computational procedure for quickly estimating readability level. *Journal of Reading Behavior, 7,* 255–267.

Slavin, R. E. (1989). PET and the pendulum: Faddism in education and how to stop it. *Phi Delta Kappan, 70,* 752–758.

Squire, J. R. (1988). Studies of textbooks: Are we asking the right questions? In P. W. Jackson (Ed.), *Contributing to educational change* (pp. 127–187). Berkeley: McCutchan.

Stein, N., & Glenn, C. (1979). An analysis of story comprehension in elementary school children. In R. Freedle (Ed.), *New directions in discourse processing* (pp. 53–120). Norwood, NJ: Ablex.

Stodolsky, S. (1989). Is teaching really by the book? In P. Jackson & S. Haroutunian-Gordon (Eds.), *From Socrates to software: The teacher as text and the text as teacher. 88th yearbook of the national society for the study of education* (Part I, pp. 159–184). Chicago: University of Chicago Press.

Sullivan, E. (1967). *Piaget and the school curriculum: A critical appraisal* (Bulletin No. 2). Ontario: Ontario Institute for Studies in Education.

Thorndike, E. (1916). An improved scale for measuring ability in reading. *Teachers College Record, 17,* 40–67.

Thorndike, E. (1921). Word knowledge in the elementary school. *Teachers College Record, 22,* 334–370.

Thorndike, E. (1931). *The teachers word book of 10,000 words.* New York: Teachers College, Columbia University.

Trombley, W. (1982, January 13). Publishers get word on more difficult textbooks. *Los Angeles Times,* pp. 1, 3, 25.

Tyson-Bernstein, H. (1988). America's textbook fiasco: A conspiracy of good intentions. *American Educator, 12*(2), 20–39.

Tyson-Bernstein, H., & Woodward, A. (1989). Nineteenth century policies for 21st century practice: The textbook reform dilemma. *Educational Policy, 3*(2), 95–106.

Vygotsky, L. (1962). *Thought and language* (E. Hanfmann & G. Vakar, Eds. & Trans.). Cambridge, MA: M. I. T. Press.

Vygotsky, L. (1978). *Mind in society* (M. Cole, V. John-Steiner, S. Scribner, & E. Souberman, Eds. & Trans.). Cambridge, MA: Harvard University Press.

Walker, D. F. (1981). Textbooks and the curriculum. In L. Cole & T. Sticht (Eds.), *The textbook in American society* (pp. 2–3). Washington, DC: Library of Congress.

Woodward, A. (1986). Textbooks: Are we getting our money's worth? In C. Cody (Ed.), *A policymaker's guide to textbook selection* (pp. 40–42). Alexandria, VA: National Association of State Boards of Education.

Yoakam, G. (1945). The reading difficulty of school textbooks. *Elementary English Review, 22,* 304–309, 333–336.

Index

157

About the Authors

JEANNE S. CHALL is Professor of Education and Director of the Reading Laboratory, Harvard University. She has written widely on reading and textbooks. She is the author of *Learning to Read: The Great Debate* and *Stages of Reading Development*, and co-author of *The Reading Crisis: Why Poor Children Fall Behind*.

SUE S. CONARD is Lecturer on Education at Harvard University, where she directs the Masters Program in Reading and Language. She has conducted research on reading materials, including the development of a scheme for the qualitative analysis of text, and co-authored the report, *An Analysis of Textbooks in Relation to Declining S.A.T. Scores*.